PARISIAN TAILS

PARISIAN TAILS

by Stephen Hayes

PARISIAN TAILS

Published 2016 by Stephen Hayes, Australia.

Artwork and original images provided by Kim Hayes

Formatted and distributed by www.ebookit.com

www.stephenhayesonline.com

ISBN: 978-0-9944590-3-9

DEDICATION

*This book is especially dedicated to my beautiful
companion Paris, but it is also dedicated to
everyone who knew her in life and have
their own fond memories of her to cherish.*

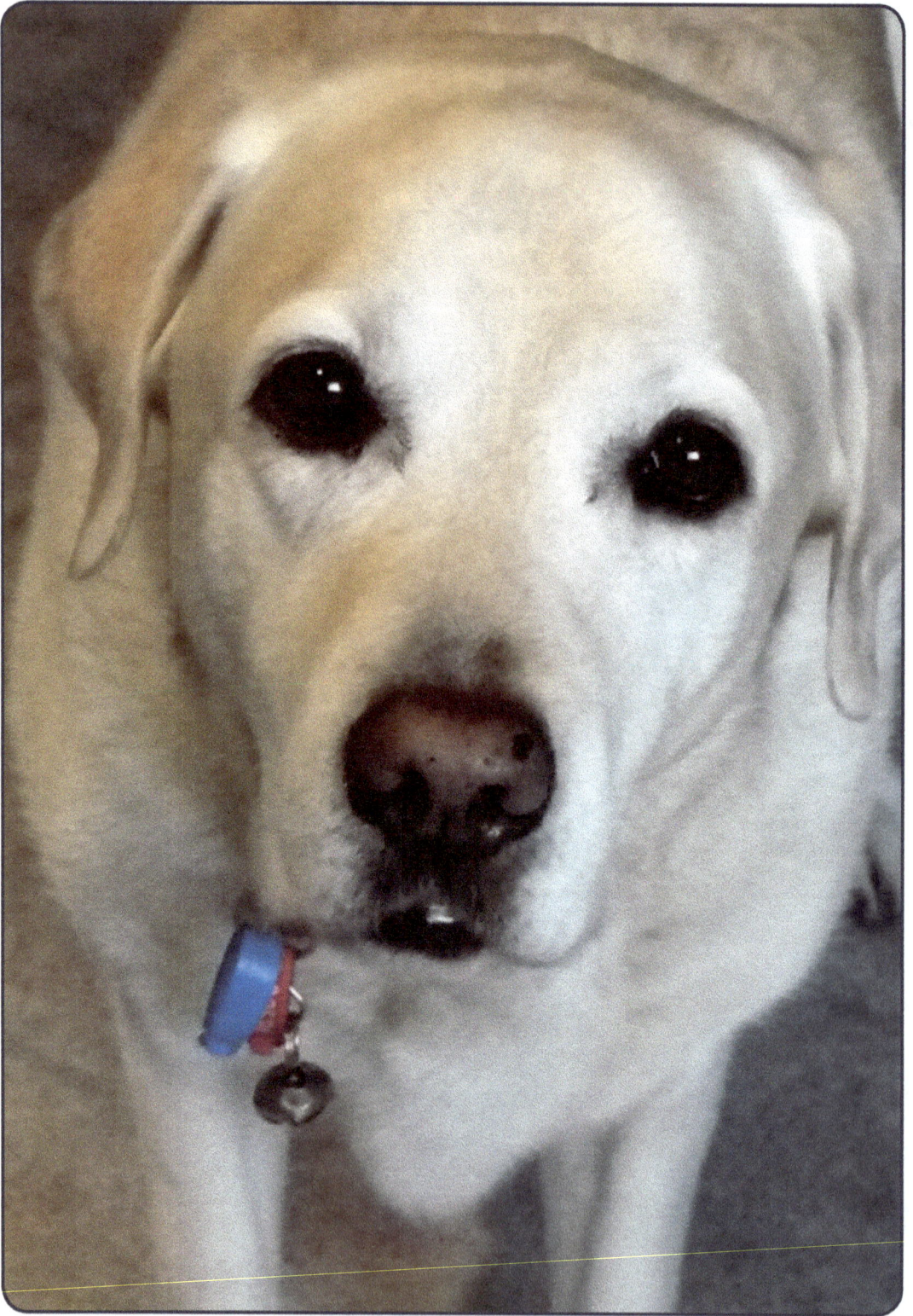

2013: Hanging round the kitchen looking her best or is it that look of feed me!

FORWARD

Dogs in this family generally don't last very long. There have been a few over Stephen's early childhood but they somehow managed to be given away to better families or they just shot through on us. So it was unexpected that Stephen went ahead and applied for a seeing-eye dog and kept his own counsel without ever revealing that one was in the wings.

Pleased as I was that he would have more mobility in the future, especially with university being a challenge in its own right where a guide-dog would be a godsend. But as with all things comes responsibility and Stephen at first assured us all that a dog would not be an issue for us as he would be the master and carer and we were to keep our distance—lest we corrupt it.

We were told a golden Labrador named Paris (from a P-litter) had been selected and Stephen would have to do intense training and do live-in's with Paris. That was fine, not a problem from our end.

At my first meeting with Paris—well, that didn't go over too well. As soon as she crossed the threshold, she saw me and barked ferociously at me while being restrained by her SEDA handler. "That'd be right", I said, "every female in the family always barks at me sooner or later in this household and this female ain't any different".

So Paris came to stay, and such was her nature we all fell head-over-heels for her. It wasn't enough that she was the 'hairy-nose' of the family but she could be very bossy in gaining attention from anyone; especially round the dinner table where she would stare down the sighted patrons and resting her drooling head on their laps while ignoring the blindies in desperate hope of gaining a morsel of food from their plates—and she often did on many occasions.

Paris had style; she had intelligence; she had a blessed way of ignoring you if it interrupted whatever she was doing. Paris was just Paris. Total love to all around her. She was unconditional and doted on the family just as much as we doted on her. She gave safety and companionship to Stephen, made best friends with his siblings Alysha and Molly and left me to pick up the crap. Sounds like a fair exchange of responsibilities.

We knew that age was catching up with her and also knew that she would someday become too ill to go on. What we didn't expect was it to be so soon. Her lethargy at the park was a tell-tale sign that something was not quite right with her and her 'menopausal' behaviour was becoming erratic. And by April 2016, Stephen became a man and made a man's decision to put Paris to bed for the last time. Such is the loss of Paris that she effected everyone that loved her because Paris is love.

—Dad, 2016

INTRODUCTION

Most people have had a pet at some stage in their lives, and in many cases, that pet would have been a dog. In some of those cases, that pet would have felt less like a pet and more like a member of the family, and even a companion. This is the story of Paris, my seeing-eye dog and best friend for nine years, who was taken from us before her time in 2016. She was truly an exceptional girl who laid her paw on the hearts of everyone she met.

We have ways of recording sound and sight into a form that others can observe through audio and video. I wish it were possible to record other things, such as touch, smell, and even thoughts themselves during certain experiences. The brain will do its best to recall the most memorable (not necessarily the best memories), but the recall won't be perfect. Over time, these memories will fade as they are replaced with new experiences.

This book is my attempt to hold onto and share as much of Paris's memory as I can. We have lots of photographs, only some of which are included in this book; as well as plenty of video footage, capturing many of her cutest moments, though missing out on plenty as well. It isn't enough for me; I would like to convey, even if it requires readers to use their imagination, just how Paris felt to the touch, and precisely how it felt to know her for nine good years.

2007: Paris at work ever alert, or is she just looking for some mischief?

THE PROCESS

As a teenager, I never thought I would get a seeing-eye dog. I always believed that I could get around quite fine with a white-cane, and that having a dog would be too much upkeep. It wasn't until the age of eighteen, while I was doing orientation and mobility (O&M) training at a TAFE institution where I would be studying the following year (so that I could get around the place independently), that I was enlightened regarding the benefits of having a seeing-eye dog.

Of those, the two main ones were the increased mobility, and the companionship. With a seeing-eye dog, it wouldn't be necessary to run my cane along walls or surfaces with edges to find my way, not if the dog knew where we were going. It wouldn't be a big issue at TAFE, but it may become one the following year, in 2007 when I would start university. As for the companionship, I took it on face-value that there may be some, but I under-estimated just how attached I would become to my first seeing-eye dog.

There was also the extra perk that guys with dogs get a little extra attention from girls, and I won't tell a lie in this story. Over the following months, as I considered whether or not to get a dog, that thought was a factor in my decision-making. I can't recall that ever happening, though, if anyone might have given me more attention because of my seeing-eye dog they inevitably were more interested in the dog than the person beside it.

I sat on it for perhaps seven or eight months before deciding that I would take the plunge and apply for a seeing-eye dog, even going as far as making notes for things to ask when I made the phone call, in case I got tongue-tied. It turned out to be very easy, though; I just had to answer some questions, sign a couple of documents, and I was immediately put on the waiting list.

A few months later, in July 2006 it would have been, I received a visit from one of the dog trainers at Seeing-Eye Dogs Australia (SEDA). For the sake of this book, let's call him Trajan; he was the same person who introduced me to the idea of getting a dog in the first place. (Trajan was the O&M instructor when I was learning my way around the TAFE the previous year.) We went over the ground rules, what I could expect, what I shouldn't expect, and what I would need to be able to do.

We then went for one of the strangest walks I have ever experienced in my life. Trajan walked in front of me and slightly to the side, and he was holding one end of a bar while I held the other end. In this manner, he guided me around the neighbourhood, all the while measuring my typical walking pace and analysing my gate and walking style. He then put me back on the waiting list where I would remain for another seven months.

In February 2007, by which time I had resigned myself to what could be a seemingly interminable wait, I received a call from another SEDA trainer (let's call her Hadrian), saying that they had found a potential dog for me — a 'lovely yellow Labrador', as she described it on my voicemail (she called me while I was in a university lecture). Two days later, I met Paris for the first time.

MEETING DAY

It was a Friday, the 2nd of March in 2007, exactly nine years to the day before Paris's final work walk. It was a beautiful sunny day and I had gotten home from university in the early afternoon in preparation. After some email correspondence with Hadrian, we agreed that I would take a little test-walk with the dog, whose name I hadn't yet been told, before making a decision on whether or not she felt right for me (such as her height, her pace, and even her personality, to a lesser extent).

Hadrian rocked up in a station wagon around three or four in the afternoon, I forget exactly when, and took me out to the car where Paris was sitting in the back. My first thought upon hearing that her name was Paris was one of hilarity, because although I was told that she was named after the city, I couldn't help comparing her, in my mind, to Paris Hilton—and the fact that she was a blonde dog didn't help that. We even joked within the family from then on that Paris's middle name ought to be Hilton.

I was strangely shy when I first met Paris. Even though she was a dog, somehow it felt like I needed to make a good first impression on her. I think I succeeded, because when she was finally standing on my driveway, panting away, I reached out to pat her—and she promptly jumped up and head-butted me in the face. Hadrian told me to tell her to sit, and she immediately obeyed me, still panting and trying to lick my hand as I patted her. She was very excitable on that first day, and she had found a very typically Paris way to break the ice.

I was shown how to put the harness on her, a process I wouldn't master until the training officially began, and then we went for our first walk together. It was immediately clear that her height was perfect for me, so that wasn't going to be an issue. She did walk a little quickly, perhaps because of her excitement, but by slowly raising and lowering the handle of the harness (a technique drilled into me during training), I was able to encourage her to temper her pace.

I wouldn't go as far as saying I fell in love with Paris on that first day, but I knew very quickly that she was the dog for me. I don't think I was necessarily anxious not to go back on the waiting list again, although I certainly didn't want to; but even if that hadn't been a factor, I still would have chosen to proceed with Paris. Not only had she demonstrated that she would be obedient (not always, but I would learn that later), but it was clear that she liked me quite as much, if not more, than I liked her.

When we returned from that first walk, Hadrian loaded Paris back into the car. (She never set foot inside my house on that first day, nor did she meet anyone else in my family.) We then talked and it was agreed that I would start my training in five weeks.

FURRY FRIEND

Even though I patted Paris's head on that first day, I didn't notice, not then at least, just how soft she was. I was more concerned with getting my own nerves under control, and making sure she wasn't going to jump up and knock my teeth out, to think about such things. I certainly would notice, though, and not before too long either. In fact, I would say that Paris's coat in general was a source of pride for me, because part of how nice it was, was down to my discipline in grooming her every day, and bathing her fairly regularly. I would attempt to memorise the feel of her in the time since, and especially in the weeks leading up to her death, so that I would never forget what I wouldn't be able to touch anymore.

While Paris had hair on her body, in most parts, it was easy to refer to it as fur—and in fact, we did that much of the time. It was especially soft on her head, which was as smooth and soft as velvet; and even more so on her ears, which were so perfectly smooth and soft if stroked downwards. My older sister Alysha would compare them to ear flaps on hats, which seemed appropriate, given that they were ear flaps. Occasionally, something small would get stuck in the hair (fur) on her head or ears, and it would always be easy to feel because of how soft and smooth they were.

Patting Paris would always be a great source of enjoyment for all of us, but Paris wouldn't always make it easy. She never bit, but she loved to lick, and she would almost always try to lick your hand when you went to pat her. Her tongue was very big, wet and slobbery. Her nose too was almost always wet; it would be dry and leathery if she had been asleep for a while, but it would usually be cold and wet, and would give you a considerable start if she came up to you and touched you with it.

It wasn't just her head and ears that were soft either; it extended to cover most of her coat. The only part of her that really wasn't 'furry' was her belly, which was pink and mostly hairless, and not a part that most people wanted to pat—although I didn't have a problem with it when I rubbed her belly. My younger sister Molly would describe the hair on her back as being like straw, and that may be on the right track; but if so, then said straw was very soft. The hair on her chest and muzzle was equally soft, and even on her snout and down her legs—although in those latter cases, the hair was shorter.

Then there was her tail—her paint-brush tail, as Alysha described it on one occasion, or an otter-like tail on another occasion. Her tail was moderately long, ending in a bit of a point. It was thick and solid, though, and quite strong when she really got wagging it. If she got excited while she was lying down, you would hear it thumping on the floor; and similarly, if I were in my bedroom and Paris in the lounge room, I would occasionally hear her tail thumping against the wall as something got her excited. It was quite normal to ask Paris to stop making such a breeze against our legs, especially over dinner time. Her tail could create such a breeze that she could sweep loose papers off a coffee table when she really got going.

ARRIVAL

Paris moved into our house on the morning of the 6th of April. We had arranged it so that I could undergo as much of my training while missing as little of my university studies as possible. Friday was Good Friday, a public holiday, and the following week was my mid-semester break, making it the ideal time to cram in as much training as possible. The usual system at SEDA (at the time) was for new trainees to move into a house they owned, and stay there with their dog for three weeks for training, but they were flexible in my case; I was able to stay in the house for only one week, and then complete the rest of my training part-time while still attending classes.

2015: Paris galloping around the park in search of a playmate of which she had many.

The arrival of Paris couldn't come soon enough for me. I was in a difficult situation at university; I had struggled through the first five weeks of it without nearly enough O&M training. Vision Australia, the most well-known vision impairment-related charity in the country, didn't have anyone available to assist me because I had left it too late to book someone. In this manner, I had missed a few classes here and there because I had been unable to find them; turned around and gone home one day because people had erected what could have passed for an obstacle course on the main thoroughfare; and actually dropped a couple of subjects because the pressure was getting to me. Things turned out to be so much better when I returned to university just over a week later with Paris at my side.

I was the one to invite Hadrian and Paris into the house for the first time, wondering what would be the first thing that Paris did once she got inside. It turned out to be something I hadn't expected at all; when my dad, with whom I live, came around the corner into the lounge room to meet her, she immediately growled at him. She would warm to him very quickly, and he would become one of her favourite people in the world before long (probably because he gave her affection without making her work as I did), but that first growl was a moment we have collectively chuckled over ever since.

The three of us (me, Paris and Hadrian) went for a good long walk on that first day, after which I was the most buggered out of the three of us. (My fitness wasn't exactly admirable at the time). The walk itself was uneventful as I remember, apart from Paris having a poo on the footpath at one stage. She only ever did that in the early stages of her working life; she was actually ridiculously-well toilet-trained, and I suppose I can thank her puppy carers for that. They sure as hell made my life a lot easier, because Paris's toileting habits were very easy to manage. She would never go in harness, after the first few weeks anyway; she would never go at university; she would almost never go when she was on the lead; and except for when she was sick, she would never go indoors (except for the pissathon, but that's several years down the track).

Afterward, Hadrian sat down with me and my dad and told us a few things about Paris that we ought to be prepared for, such as the fact that Paris would need some time to adjust to her new surroundings, and that there may be some unusual behavior in that time, such as sloppy poos and chewing on things; but that it would settle down before long and things would be fine. This turned out to be the case; Paris only pooed two more times on training walks that I can remember, and after that, everything was golden (except for the Southern Cross incident, but that's still to come as well).

As for the chewing, she did do a bit of that in the early days, such as ruining a good pair of headphones I had left on my bed while staying at the SEDA house, running off with a roll of toilet paper and making a mess of it through the house, and completely destroying a plastic stubby holder I drank soft drink out of and making an almighty mess of it under my desk. I was pretty annoyed at her for that, and actually gave her the cold shoulder for an hour or two, but in the end, she was rubbing herself against my legs and practically begging for my forgiveness, so I had to let her know that it was okay.

BONDING WEEKEND

I had another brief training session on Easter Saturday, but it was a much shorter walk this time. Paris and I were then left to our devices until Tuesday, when the two of us would go into the SEDA house for seven days. Before we were left alone, though, Hadrian brought me up on a couple of things I'd been doing wrong regarding Paris the previous evening. Firstly, as I'd been nervous that Paris wouldn't come to me when I called her, I had left her lead attached so that it would be easier to catch her if I had to. There were two things wrong with this: Paris might chew on it, and she might get tangled up in it, fortunately neither of which happened that night. It turned out not to be a problem, though, because Paris usually did come when I called her; and if she didn't, it usually wouldn't be too difficult to go and get her.

Secondly, as a seeing-eye dog, Paris couldn't think that she could be allowed on the furniture, because it might make her think she could get on anyone's furniture. I had let Paris curl up and sleep in one of the armchairs in our family room prior to dinner on the Friday night without realising it was against the rules, just happy that she was comfortable and behaving herself. The funny thing about that was according to Hadrian, who had trained Paris herself, Paris knew the rules, but was happy to try to bend them wherever she could.

That was one other thing Hadrian did before leaving me and Paris to our own devices: She filled me in on what she knew about Paris's personality. For instance, Paris would always try to please me and to make me proud of her when we were working. I noticed that because whenever she did something right while we were walking together, and I let her know that she had done well, I would feel her tail brushing my arm as she wagged it higher into the air. Another part of her personality I was told of, was her cheekiness; she was a very smart dog, but she would still try to break the rules if she thought she could get away with it. Her continually testing the boundaries would be a regular theme throughout her life, especially when it came to food.

Another thing Paris loved to do, from the day we met to the day she died, was sleep under things, as if it were her own little cubbyhole. My desk and the kitchen table were regulars, but by far her favourite spot was under my dad's bed, which was just high enough for her to get in, but still so low that she would have bumped her head every time she raised it. To this day, I wish that she could have gotten under my bed, but the bed I had for the entire time I had Paris was too low to the floor for her to fit. When she could get away with it, she would occasionally try to sleep on my dad's bed, and would quickly jump down whenever she was caught as if to say, "Who, me? You didn't see what you think you just saw." But the paw prints she left on the bed always gave her away.

The rest of that long weekend was spent bonding, not just between me and Paris but also my dad and Alysha as well, the latter of whom didn't immediately take to the new family member. She made a rule that Paris could never go into her bedroom, and made sure that she always closed her door when she wasn't in there, so that any dog smell wouldn't pervade her room. It didn't take too long for Paris to lick and wet-nose her way into Alysha's heart, though, just as she did with most people she met.

There was little to worry about, anyway, because Paris didn't really have much of a smell most of the time—at least in the early days. Granted, my bedroom, where Paris slept every night until 2014, would soon be defined by a canine smell that no air-freshener could defeat; but when she was clean, Paris didn't really have a dog smell at all. If anything, all her coat smelt like was just that: A fur coat. She would only get smelly if she had been recently licked by other dogs, or if she hadn't been bathed in a while. In the early days, she could go as much as a couple of months without a bath; then as time wore on, that interval decreased until in the last eighteen months or so, she would be a little smelly a week after having a bath.

There was one other thing that Hadrian showed (or told) me how to do before leaving—I can't remember if it was demonstrated or if I figured it out myself. That was Paris's feeding regimen, which was specifically strict so that Paris, being a Labrador, would be kept in line, both in terms of her weight and her discipline while out working. It involved filling a cup of her food, of which SEDA had provided the first bag; tipping it into a bowl, which SEDA had also provided; and then blowing a whistle to tell Paris to eat, after making sure that she was dutifully sitting before the bowl and obediently not eating it.

This process had to be done twice a day, and my routine quickly revolved around it. I would get up in the morning (around six o'clock, as that was the time Paris came to expect), let Paris out to go to the toilet, and then ready her breakfast. Then in the evening, I would give her her dinner as soon as I had finished my own, assuming we were at home and it were possible to do so. If we weren't, I would usually feed Paris as soon as we got home, even though SEDA told me I wasn't supposed to do that (in case she came to expect food every time we got home, no matter the time of day). This was one of the few rules I broke, mostly because it was just easier for me, and Paris was quite happy to go along.

IN DA HOUSE

On the 10th of April, I met yet another SEDA trainer—let's call this one Antonius. He drove me and Paris to the SEDA house, where we lived until the 17th, and it was he who trained us during that time. The majority of the training was neighbourhood walks, both around the house and in neighbouring suburbs, so that Paris and I would have some variety to work with, and things would be less predictable. The three most memorable incidents I can recall taking place on these walks were: Walking me smack-bang into a post box, walking past the front door of the house several times in a row (as if she didn't want to finish walking yet), and very sneakily leading me towards another dog without me realising it until they were already very close.

One of the trainers (I don't recall which one) told me that seeing-eye dogs would typically test their new owners during the training process. I even recall Trajan telling me during our meeting the previous year of one dog who walked its owner past the house no less than twenty times, testing him all the while. The key was to not lose one's temper at the seeing-eye dog, but to be firm all the same. So when Paris decided to pull that same stunt on me, I was at least prepared to deal with it (once Antonius told me each time that we walked past the front door anyway).

As for incidents like the post box, there would be many similar to those, not just during the training process but all through Paris's working life. There were two main causes of this: Paris could get very easily distracted, and she could sometimes see a narrow gap which she could fit through, but would forget to calculate me into whatever passed for an equation in her mind. In that particular incident, I hit my right shoulder pretty hard, and Antonius told me to correct Paris as firmly as I could (which sometimes involved a sharp pull on the harness, or a sharp pull on the lead, depending on the circumstances), and then to take her back and try walking through the same place again; and repeat until Paris got it right, at which point I would praise and pat her before continuing.

When I first got Paris, SEDA provided me with a half-choker collar that was meant to be used during training. Due to Paris's tendency to get distracted, however, Antonius brought over a full-choker collar in which I could train Paris until we got her mind firmly back on the job. Since Paris always walked on my left, this only really applied if the distraction was on our left (as if it were on our right, I would feel her try to cross in front of my body, and I could just nudge her with my leg to get her back on the job). The half-choker was only metallic around the front, while the full-choker was entirely metallic, but Paris didn't seem to mind wearing them. She would be much more objectionable to the nose grip, but that would come later.

It wasn't just walking, though. We also did obedience training before and after walks, while the rest of the time was time off for me, during which I was supposed to bond and get used to living with Paris. This was very easy because we were fortunate enough to be the only two beings in that house for most of the time we were there. In this time, I would learn that Paris would usually sit when told to do so, especially if I put my hand on her rump and gently pushed; and in the same way, she would lie down if I commanded "down" and put my hand on the back of her neck.

I didn't spend every waking moment with Paris while I was in the house; I would also listen to music and spend time on the Internet, using a dial-up modem that was old-fashioned even back in 2007. It was during these times that I was at the desk in the large living room that I taught Paris a very important lesson, which would benefit me for many years to come. When Paris wanted attention, one of her signature ways to get it was to stick her nose under a person's arm and raise it in a way that was just about impossible to ignore, and you'd better hope you weren't holding a drink when it happened or you could say goodbye to it, and whatever clothes you were wearing at the time.

I demonstrated to Paris, every single time she tried this, that when I was busy with something, there was nothing that she could do to distract me. She quickly learned to stop trying, making it easier for me to concentrate on schoolwork later on. It took a lot of self-discipline to make this work, though, as I couldn't help feeling a little guilty every time I deliberately ignored my doggy. I made myself get up and play with Paris not too long after this, letting her know that I wasn't really ignoring her; but at the same time, our time together would be on my terms, not hers.

As for playing, it was a good place to do it because there was a lot of space. SEDA gave me two toys when I first got Paris, both of which would disappear before too long, but Paris would have many more in the years to come. There was a hard-rubbery thing called a kong, which was oddly-shaped and would bounce very unpredictably. It was hard enough so that Paris wouldn't be able to chew through it, as she proved she would do with any toy made of rubber in the years to come. The kong would eventually find its way into the back yard because my dad didn't want it to leave marks on the walls. We did play fetch with it, but ultimately, Paris wouldn't be as interested in the kong as the other toy.

And that was a rope, braded along its length and tied in a large knot at each end. The first rope she got was quite small, and it eventually disappeared somewhere in our backyard at home, but it would be replaced by longer ropes, which would fray over time as Paris's teeth wore them down. I would throw the rope down the long hallway towards the front door in the SEDA house, and Paris would sprint after it and bring it back, like the retriever dog she was. She wouldn't be content to just give it back, though, because there was one game she enjoyed much more than fetch: tug-of-war.

She wasn't particularly good at tug-of-war when we played it in the SEDA house because through most of the house, apart from the bedrooms (which weren't big enough to play in), the floors were made of hard wood (easier to clean up all the dog hair, I assume). She would try to dig her nails in, but she wouldn't be able to get any kind of purchase, and so tug-of-war at that time was basically me pulling Paris around the living room while she slipped and slid all over the floor, trying as hard as she could to pull back.

We never played outside, though. In fact, we rarely played outside at all, but we didn't do it at all in the SEDA house—because I never learnt my way around out there. It turned out to be a bit of a problem because Paris would sometimes decide not to come back inside when I called her, and I would have to leave her out there for half an hour or more before she would finally come in. She tried pulling this stunt when we were about to go out for a walk, and Antonius actually threw his keys at her to get her to move. Not only did it fail to move her, but he had to go out and look for his keys, so suffice it to say we got off to a late start that day.

On the 16th, the day before Paris and I would return home, someone else moved into the SEDA house. I can't remember her name, but she wasn't another client training with a dog, but rather someone working with SEDA who had come from interstate and was staying for a few days. We only met once, on the Monday morning, as she was out all that day and came home after I had gone to bed that night. She left the following morning after I had gone back to bed (after getting up to feed Paris while she was still in bed). Even though I was in bed, though, I knew exactly when she got home, and when she left the next morning; all thanks to Paris, who must have thought there was an intruder in the house and barked so loudly in the enclosed space of my bedroom that I practically flew out of bed to quieten her.

It's a wonder she didn't give me a heart-attack on those two occasions, especially since I'd been asleep both times, because although Paris couldn't have been a gentler, friendlier dog, she had a very aggressive-sounding bark. That would be another characteristic that would last until the end. When Paris barked at you, it would sound like she wanted to rip your throat out, when all she really wanted to do was sniff your pants and lick your face. She wouldn't bark a lot, but heaven help anyone who had the audacity to come near our house while Paris was looking out the window, and especially if they had the nerve to come up to the front door and knock or ring the bell.

2012: Paris getting annoyed by my affections.

Antonius offered to end the in-house training a day early, in case I didn't want to share the house with this other person, but I rejected the offer. I can't remember why, because I do remember feeling a bit annoyed that I would have to share with another person, after having it to myself all that time. Perhaps I came to my senses and realised that I'd been quite fortunate to have it to myself that whole time, or perhaps I realised that I wouldn't have to see this other person much anyway, or perhaps I just wanted to go through with the process as we had planned it. Whatever it was, the in-house training ended on the 17th of April, and Paris and I returned home to continue the training in part-time mode with Hadrian.

GRADUATION

Paris and I continued our training for another six or seven weeks—I can't remember the exact date of her graduation except that I'm pretty sure it was a week day in early June of 2007. Her graduation ceremony was about as modest as you can possibly imagine; it simply consisted of Hadrian handing me a certificate to say that Paris was a fully qualified seeing-eye dog, and that was it. It took place in our family room at home, and no one other than me, Hadrian and Paris herself was there to see it.

The majority of the training that took place over that six or seven weeks was around the university campus, or on the way to or from it. The route I took to get to the campus involved a twenty-minute walk from home to a nearby tram stop, a short tram trip, and then the walk up through the university itself. We never bothered to train her on a train (pun intended) or a bus, and in fact, I don't recall Paris ever needing to work on either of those forms of public transport in her entire life.

I can't remember most of the training we did in that time, but there were a few notable incidents, including the last time I can recall Paris doing a poo while she was supposed to be working (apart from the Southern Cross incident, but that's still to come). There was also an incident when we were about to get on the tram at the university, on our way home, and just as we were about to do so, Paris turned and started trying to hurry off to the left. Hadrian had been trying to hide from Paris so that she wouldn't be distracted, but she had to come into view so that she wouldn't miss the tram and lose us; and Paris tried to go over to her as soon as she saw her. I don't think we missed the tram that day, but I can't remember for certain. All I do remember is that Hadrian had to help me get Paris's mind back on the job.

That wasn't the only tram incident either. One time towards the end of the training, on a trip where Hadrian was not actually on the tram with us but had taken the previous one and was waiting on the other side of road for me and Paris to arrive, Paris and I almost failed to get off the tram at all. It was peak-time and the tram was full of people, a great many of them fellow students, and Paris and I hadn't been able to get our usual seat close to the front—or any seat close to the front, as it turned out. We had ended up sitting near a door in the middle of the tram, but when we had tried to get off, the driver hadn't seen us, and had shut the doors just as Paris and I were descending the steps, so that poor Paris ended up jammed right up against the doors. Thankfully the other passengers saw what had happened and yelled for the driver to open the doors again. Even more thankfully, neither of us were hurt.

I can only recall one other memorable experience during training, and it wasn't a particularly good one—though thankfully, it only lasted for a few seconds. It happened in one of the computer labs during a tutorial. Someone was there with me; it may have been Hadrian or it may have been someone from the Disability Unit taking notes for me. Either way, with not a lot of space underfoot, and me juggling a laptop, a bag and a dog, it got rather cramped. I pushed back from the desk, perhaps to get something from my bag, which I'd put at my feet, and one of the wheels of the spinning chair went over Paris's tail. She made a loud gasping panting sound for about a second or two before I rolled forward again, horrified by what I'd done, but at least she hadn't yelped.

Paris normally would yelp if someone stepped on her tail—a horrible sound that really pierced the heart. Well, it had that effect on me anyway. Fortunately, it only ever happened a handful of times, such as once when my dad's partner at the time accidentally put her heel down on Paris's tail (that had been Paris's fault because the silly doggy kept getting under people's feet). I did it myself once, while I was brushing her; I leaned forward on my knees so that I could reach around her better, and one of my knees came down on her tail. Each time that happened, Paris must have been in some pain, and her response would be to get up and skitter about for a bit. I had to settle her down each time that happened.

But it was thanks to Paris that I was able to get around the university much more easily. Once I had orientation training (usually with my dad, because I'd lost faith in Vision Australia's reliability), she was able to get me to wherever my classes were, and the most trouble we ever had was caused by large crowds of people who didn't always watch where they were going. In turn, it meant that I could set my mind on the studies themselves, and was able to get very good grades (in 2007 anyway). I may have dropped out of university in 2010 without finishing the course, but I still largely thank Paris for helping me do so well that year.

THE DESTROYER

Anyone who has ever known a Labrador will be familiar with how quickly and easily they can wreck things. I hadn't been aware of their reputation when I first got Paris (I had only been aware of their tendency to drop hair everywhere). As time went on, I began to think of Paris as 'the destroyer', because it seemed like she would destroy everything she touched. Not only had she caused me to have to go out and buy a good pair of headphones, and that horrendous stubby holder incident (I got a new one for my birthday later in the year, which Paris kept her teeth off, thank heavens), but there were other things too.

She was very well toilet trained, and only when she was sick did she go in the house, but what she wasn't trained to do was let me know when she was about to vomit. Paris's vomiting was something I didn't enjoy at all, and for quite a few reasons. Firstly, it was horrible to listen to; it was a loud, deep belching sound that would happen four or five times, followed by an even yuckier sound which, at the time, I thought was Paris trying to lick up her own spew; but in fact was probably just her pushing the vomit out of her mouth with her tongue.

Hearing that was bad, but not hearing it was worse, because it meant that I would either step in it, or if I happened to smell it first (a high enough probability, as it was pretty damn stinky, thanks mostly to the food she ate), I would have to feel around for it with my hands so that I wouldn't step in it later. Then there was the stain it left on the carpet. Paris would leave a lot of vomit stains on the carpet throughout the house—mostly in my bedroom, as she seemed to like saving the vomiting episodes for the middle of the night most of the time. The carpets were cleaned several times throughout Paris's lifetime, but it didn't change the fact that she was leaving her mark.

Then there was the back yard. Paris continually did a number on our back yard, despite my dad's best attempts to keep it under his control. He put up a small fence on the lawn, which lasted 12–18 months, so that Paris could only access a small part of it on which to do her toileting. It didn't take her long to kill the grass there, of course, but it wasn't enough for Paris, who wanted to run around on the rest of the grass and sniff out the garden. She was able to dig her way under the fence, between it and the boundary fence, and was soon killing the grass on the rest of the lawn. Later on, when my dad retired and started doing more with the garden, Paris would come along after him and taste-test whatever he was growing there, and it was in this way that she learned that tomatoes didn't taste so good when they hadn't ripened.

Then there were her toys. We never bought soft stuffed toys for Paris because she would chew them up and spread the stuffing around the room in short order, as happened whenever someone was foolish enough to get her one. She had various rubber toys over the duration, most of which she eventually wrecked (apart from the last couple, but she became less interested in playing in the last year of her life). When she did chew up a rubber toy, it would usually be because she was bored, or because we were sitting around chatting and Paris wanted to be around us, so she would just lie on the floor and chew up her toys while she listened to us. When she did chew up her rubber toys, she left behind a great big mess that the vacuum cleaner would have to take care of later.

And then there were her ropes—her favourite toys, which she made a mess of every time she played with them. Sometimes she would chew them up just as she would with the rubber toys, and they wouldn't last very long when that happened, but it didn't necessarily have to be chewing. Tug-of-war was her favourite game, and when we played it, bits of rope would go flying every time she lost—as her teeth would inevitably pull bits of thread out. So pretty much every time I played with her, she would leave some sort of mess behind.

SEPARATION

It's generally accepted that a seeing-eye dog goes everywhere with its handler, that is why we have laws saying that seeing-eye dogs must be granted entry into any and all establishments. However, there were times when taking Paris somewhere, while technically allowed, would have been too difficult, and presented far more trouble than it would have been worth. While I knew this from the beginning, my thoughts had been initially to take her anyway, and to put up with the trouble, because I was concerned that Paris would get up to mischief if we left her at home. I was also concerned that it wouldn't be such a good idea to leave the back door open the entire time that I was gone, even though the alternative was risking her dropping something unpleasant on the carpet.

We got our first chance to test this in May, 2007, before Paris had even graduated. Going to the football with my dad was something I enjoyed doing maybe half a dozen times a year, and when we decided to go to this particular game, I suggested bringing Paris along. I wasn't worried about her being put off by the noise (Paris would ultimately prove that loud noises didn't bother her), but was eventually turned off the idea by the lack of space (Paris probably would have been stepped on by people trying to get to their seats, unless we stood at the back of the stands for the whole match, which I didn't want to do).

On that day, we left Paris at home on her own, shutting her out of the house but leaving the door at the back of the garage open so that if she wanted to go under cover (if it rained, for example), she would be able to. At some point while we were gone, however, the wind blew this door shut, and unfortunately it shut Paris inside the garage for the remainder of the afternoon. She would have been bored, and may have wrecked the back yard if she could have (that part which she could access at the time, anyway), but instead she ended up making an almighty mess of the garage.

As it turned out, the mistake we made was to put Paris through that so early on in her time with us. For a while after that, someone (often Alysha) would babysit (or dog-sit, if you prefer) while we were gone. After a while, though, even this wouldn't be strictly necessary; if left to her own devices for up to a few hours, Paris could easily go and lie down on her bed or somewhere else in the house, and simply have a sleep until we returned. Normally, she wouldn't even need to go to the toilet in this time; her need would only really increase if she either ran around a lot, or drank a lot.

I never really liked leaving her alone, though. On the occasions when I had to, my mind would always flick regularly to Paris, hoping that she was doing okay. Then when I returned, one of the first things I would always do was go and check on her and give her a good pat. Quite often, I wouldn't have to go far, as Paris would hear the car pull up and be waiting with her nose pressed against the door for us to open it from the other side.

I'm also given to understand that on at least one occasion, Paris herself pined for me while I was away. One afternoon, again while we were at the football (I can't remember exactly when this was), Alysha was dog-sitting again, and she told me later that Paris wandered into my bedroom at one stage through the afternoon, as if she were looking for me, and then wandered out again, whining a little. So although Paris usually handled herself fine when left alone, perhaps she found her own mind flicking to me in the same way mine continually flicked to her—I can imagine so anyway.

Of course, when it came to leaving Paris alone, I would only be comfortable doing it during the day, and only if I could be sure that she had access to her water, and a place to go to the toilet. I put my foot down in the evening, though, because Paris quickly settled into a routine that involved having dinner sometime between half past five and seven o'clock in the evening, and usually after we humans had finished eating. If we went out for dinner, I would take Paris with me wherever we ended up going (unless it was the football again, in which case I would either feed her before I left or leave it to the dog-sitter to do). It wasn't just the food, though; I just didn't feel comfortable leaving Paris all alone at night time.

INTERSTATE

Paris went on her first holiday with me in July, 2007. Well, perhaps holiday is the wrong word, as she did spend a fair amount of the time in harness. It was her first interstate trip, anyway (unless she went interstate before I got her, but I honestly don't know if that happened), and one of only two times she and I would leave Victoria together. On this occasion, it was to attend the National Braille Music Camp, a week of singing and mingling with other blind people. In fact, Paris was one of five seeing-eye dogs there that week, although I was the only male who brought a dog along.

Even on camp, though, I didn't take Paris everywhere I went—although I did take her with me most of the time. The 'singing room', however, was not something I wanted to expose her to; it was a classroom which had been packed with no less than seventy-five chairs, more than it was designed for, and then crammed with everyone who attended the camp. If Paris had gone in there, she would have been stepped on, I'm certain of it, and so the three times a day when we had to squeeze into that room, I left Paris back in my own bedroom, where she just slept until I returned.

Although she wasn't the only dog there, she did become fairly popular, perhaps because she was so friendly or because she had the softest coat out of all of them— I'm not sure. All I know is one night mid-way through the camp, a couple of people took Paris around so that other people could meet and pat her—I stressed a little over where she was until she was returned to me about twenty minutes later. She was also popular with one of the other dogs, Bonnie; she and Paris continually tried to walk towards each other throughout the week, as though they had a bit of a doggy friendship happening.

Paris did get up to mischief a couple of times, though, and both of them involved getting loose. The first time this happened was on the very first day, on the train that was taking us from Melbourne to Mittagong, the location of the camp (at least nine hours of travel time). I had gone to the toilet, and while I was in there, Paris slipped out of the compartment I was sharing with a friend, and gone wandering up the carriage; it took about five minutes to catch her and bring her back.

The second time it happened was a few days in, during one afternoon when I had taken Paris off the lead so that she could wander around within the confines of the lounge room. When someone opened the outside door, however, Paris managed to slip through, and it was very difficult to get her to come back, no matter how many times I called to her, and no matter how much ferocity I packed into the calls. Even when one of my friends retrieved her food whistle from my bedroom, she still wouldn't come despite the fact that she's supposed to come when she hears the whistle. The same friend even went back to get a small portion of food to tempt

Paris, but by the time she returned, Paris had finally come back to me, perhaps realising that she was in trouble and had better do as she's told.

The greatest concern I had regarding Paris on camp, though, was her toileting. I wasn't wild about picking up her droppings, but I was even more worried that she wouldn't do any droppings, just like she wouldn't do anything at university. That turned out to be the case; I didn't dare let her off the lead to go to the toilet, and with me standing beside her, walking her around on the grass, she simply refused to go. She probably urinated a few times (she would have exploded otherwise), but she never dropped a number-two, and I know it because I had the unpleasant job of crouching down and feeling around on the grass to see if she had.

I couldn't do anything about it, though, and I won't lie in this book: Part of me was glad I didn't have to pick up after her. But the laws of physics suggest you can't keep putting stuff into a dog and have nothing coming back out of the dog—it just doesn't work, and so it didn't. Paris stubbornly held on until the train pulled into Southern Cross Station in Melbourne, but when the train doors opened and she saw my dad on the other side of them, she bounded through, dragging me with her, to say hello to him.

It was her excitement that brought about the fabled 'Southern Cross' incident that night, in which Paris dropped into a squat as we were walking across the platform, dropping one of the smelliest poos I've ever known in my life, and in front of countless people. Poor dad had to pick it up and dispose of it, and then we had to walk the rest of the way out of the station. I couldn't see Paris, of course, but I imagine she was looking shame-faced as we went.

THE RUG

Paris slowly but surely became a member of the family throughout the second half of 2007, and it was during this time that she would acquire some of her first nicknames. Paris would end up having lots of nicknames, and she would respond to all of them—not necessarily because she recognized the words, although she may have done, but because she had a good sense of when she was being addressed—or even when she was being talked about. On one occasion, while I was walking either to or from uni (I forget which), when crossing a road, instead of using the typical "forward" command, I said "go doggy go"; and like a good seeing-eye dog, Paris went doggy went.

My dad's early nickname for Paris was Il Pooché, which would eventually give way to be replaced by his preferred nickname, Hairy Nose. I would often refer to her as the French Wanderer, which I would shorten to Frenchy on occasions. Alysha would have many nicknames for her including Princess Paris, Her Furriness and Labradorable, though when she was patting her and Paris was trying to lick her, she would call her "Doggydoggydoggydoggydoggy". There would be others as well, many given to her in light of her behaviour, but the one that makes me smile the most to this day is 'The Rug'.

That particular nickname first came about in July 2007, when the three of us (me, my dad and Alysha), were reading 'Harry Potter and the Deathly Hallows' as a family, so that we wouldn't have to wait until it was available in audio format and run the risk of having it spoilt by those who had already read it. While the chapters were being read, Paris would be lying somewhere close by, imitating a rug. Sometimes she would be in front of or beside one of us, sometimes in a position where we could rest our feet on her. Other times she would be under the kitchen table, imitating a rug as she slept, even interrupting one chapter with a yipping doggy dream.

She never shook off this nickname because that part of her character never changed. She was a playful dog, but being a Labrador, she would always be ready to lie down and have a sleep somewhere. If she wanted peace and quiet, she would go to her bed in my bedroom or under my dad's bed, but a lot of the time, she would spread herself out beside one of us so that even while she had a nap (or just lay there), she would be near a person. I really enjoyed it when she came and lay beside my chair while I was working, or down at my feet so that I could rest them on her like a nice…rug.

2008: Paris and I stayed still long enough for this pose.

PARIS, THE SOCIALITE

As already stated, Paris was a very friendly dog. Whenever she met a new person, even if she initially barked at them, she would always want to go and investigate them; familiarize herself with their smell; and give them a good licking to boot. If this meeting were to take place anywhere outside of the house where she spent the vast majority of her life, Paris would dispense with the barking, but would still want to thoroughly introduce herself. She would only draw away from a person if, after checking them out, she got a sense that they weren't a dog person.

Her friendly and inquisitive nature would cause me a whole lot of problems over the years. In fact, it's fair to say that throughout her working life, I was never able to train her not to get distracted by things around her. If someone tried to pat her, even while she was working, she would be all too willing to allow herself to be patted. If she saw another dog, she would try to drag me in that direction—or at the very least whine about it. Even if she heard a dog barking behind a fence as we walked past, she would whine a bit, as though she wanted to go and say hello.

The only exception to this was a dog which lived about a block away; whenever we passed that house, that dog would growl at her and she would growl back, wanting to drag me over to the fence and stick her nose up against it. It would take some effort to get her to move on, but before long, I would be ready to drag her away before we had even reached that house. That behaviour continued well after I suspect that other dog to have gone; either Paris believed it was still there, or it had left a lingering smell for a long time afterwards.

But Paris wasn't just a seeing-eye dog; she was also a pet, and we made sure that she got plenty of opportunities to socialise with other dogs, without having to worry about being in harness. Allowing dogs to run free was an important component in having a seeing-eye dog, according to SEDA, who gave me a whole lesson on how I should go about taking a dog free-running: Never walk the dog to the park in harness, never go anywhere near the park while working the dog, always take the whistle and a bit of food just in case you have trouble getting the dog to come back. I really only took one lesson from all of this—to take Paris free-running only if you have someone sighted to accompany you.

There were several parks in the general neighbourhood that allowed dogs to go free-running. The first one we took her to was the biggest, but it also had a creek, and after Paris decided to go for a swim a few times, we in turn decided to find a different park. The one which she would eventually frequent in the last four-or-five years of her life was a football/cricket field with a footpath around it, which my dad and I would lap a couple of times while Paris frolicked in the grass, sniffing everything in sight. Occasionally, that park would be used for a cricket match while we were down there, so we would go to another park instead. And in the last couple of years, Paris would find yet another park to run in while I was being tortured by my personal trainer.

Paris loved these free-runs. It was great for her if she could just run around and sniff the grass, but it was even better when there were dogs

to play with—large dogs especially. Paris could get on with any dog, but the smaller dogs weren't particularly interested in her—they would go all Napoleon complex on her, which was ironic given what country Napoleon came from. Whenever Paris and a dog got together in the park, the usual butt-sniffing introductions would ensue, followed by lots of chasing and tail-wagging. Paris would meet and play with lots of dogs during these runs, most of whom she only met once or twice, but a few with whom she would become good mates.

THE CHRISTMAS DOGGY

Paris would spend a total of nine Christmases in our family. Some were more memorable than others, but those which were memorable will live on in infamy. Paris loved Christmas, and not just because she would get a few new toys to destroy, nor because of all the wonderful smells coming from Christmas lunch and dessert and whatever else was going on in the kitchen—although that was certainly part of it. Paris loved it because she quickly learned how to unwrap her own presents with her teeth, and for her, tearing off the wrapping paper and spreading it around the floor to get to the veritable candy in the centre was often more fun than playing with the presents themselves.

Her typical presents were little doggy treats (often a certain brand name, who shall remain nameless unless they pay me to mention them), ropes, rubber toys, and occasionally stuffed toys which she quickly tore to shreds. One thing she rarely got were bones, and I would be hit with anxiety every time she did. This was because in 2007, one such bone made her quite sick, causing her to vomit and then do a poo in my bedroom—the only time she did that in her entire life—until the very end, anyway.

And when they didn't make her sick, they made her fart a lot. On one such night, after she had stunk up the lounge room, my dad forced her to come into my room, where I had to open the window all the way, despite the fact that it was winter, just so that I wouldn't suffocate. I maintained for a long time that the stench of Paris's farts could be weaponized in the right concentration, and it would inspire me in the creation of a scene in one of my other books, 'Corridors', where the smell of farts (not specifically dog farts) was used in such a way.

But those weren't the only memories Paris created at Christmas times, nor were they what she became most notorious for. It wasn't the Christmas scarf we occasionally wrapped around her neck, nor was it the one time when she busted right through the back sliding door at my aunt's house while we were eating Christmas lunch, knocking it clean off its rails and onto the floor with an almighty crash. It wasn't even the time in 2014 when she crept through the kitchen while everyone was preparing Christmas lunch, going unnoticed, right up until she stuck her face in the bowl of couscous, gobbled it all down without anyone noticing but that pales compared to earlier Christmases.

It was the left-over chicken on the bench—not once, but twice. In 2007, after we had finished eating Christmas dinner at my mum's place, the left-over chicken had been placed on the bench. Molly turned away for no more than 30 seconds, and when she turned back, the chicken was gone, and Paris was licking her lips, quite happy with herself. We laughed about that for a long time, and that laughter only increased two years later when, once again after Christmas dinner at my mum's place, my younger brother Zac (who lived with her) was asked to go and checked to make sure that Paris hadn't eaten the left-over chicken on the bench. When he returned and told us that she had, we didn't believe him right away, but he was telling the truth.

Suffice it to say, Paris got very small dinners on those nights. They were far from the only times Paris got her chops around food that she wasn't supposed to—I can think of several others, and quite a few of those times, the food was given to her by naughty humans—but those two Christmas dinners were the most memorable.

2010: Paris in the Christmas spirit, NOT!

GREAT COMPANIONSHIP

The first half of 2008 saw things change for me personally. It was my second year of university and the work became considerably more difficult. It was the first time I realised just how unlikely it was that I would succeed in an IT career, as I had been imagining since high school (I was no more talented than anyone else in my class, in a seemingly saturated market, and in fact, due to my blindness, I may be more a liability for future employers who could probably get better quality work from an easier-to-hire sighted employee). Given how hard I'd worked to get to this point, I began to burn out, and in the end, I gave up trying to keep up.

One result of this was that I got quite a lot of writing done in that time (this was a time when writing was still a hobby for me, although I was working on 'Hunt and Power' by then). Another result of this, though, was a new and increased bond with Paris. I didn't work her as much as I'd done the previous year, although I did still take her for walks around the neighbourhood (just to keep up the practice), but it wasn't the working that brought us closer: It was the play time.

Paris loved her tug-of-war, and she and I would play plenty of that game in that time. When I needed a break from writing, or whatever else I happened to be doing, Paris would be there, and she and I would get on the floor and wrestle. She was very strong, and she would really dig her nails into the carpet for purchase. She would also shake her head from side-to-side in an effort to shake the rope loose from her opponent, which was often enough to beat other people who weren't used to her, but I learned how to deal with her.

For starters, it was always important to hold on tight. This was usually easy, although sometimes the silly dog would pick the rope up in the middle and expect to play tug-of-war, which really made things more difficult. I could make things more difficult for her by also shaking the rope from side-to-side, but like me, Paris quickly learnt to hold on tight. It would be unpleasant if you accidentally let go, especially if she was shaking her head. If you were lucky, her own momentum would send her flying backward out of harm's way. If you weren't lucky, as I wasn't on one memorable occasion, the knotted end of the rope would swing around and hit you in the face—that made me see stars.

I enjoyed this game a lot, especially when Paris fought with all she had. Sometimes she would stay on the defensive, but I learnt another trick to change that. By measuring the strength of my pulling to match her own, I would hold her at a stalemate for several seconds before giving up just a little—enough for her to think she was getting the better of me. Once she got that idea in that rock-hard head of hers, she would go into full-on shake-the-hell-out-of-this-thing mode, sending me back on the defensive.

Eventually, though, I would need to either win or lose just to get my breath back. There were two effective ways to beat Paris at this game. One was to attempt to put her in a headlock while not letting go of the rope; you wouldn't need to succeed for her to quickly let go of the thing. The other was to try to tickle her front toes with your free hand; she didn't like that. If she could, she would try to fold her front legs in under her body so that you couldn't reach her toes, and doing this would often be enough to distract her and cause her to let go of the rope.

When I won the game, which I almost always did, I would throw the rope for her to go and fetch, like the good retriever dog she was. Usually, she would go and get it, but sometimes she would either play dumb or—well to be honest, I don't know exactly what went through her head in these times. All I knew was that she would come back to me, no rope in mouth, and I would give her a big cuddle. This usually ended up with her flopping onto her back and me giving her a belly-rub as she rolled around on the floor with her legs waving in the air.

COUSINS AND FRIENDS

You know by now what a friendly, sociable doggy Paris was, but that sociable behaviour didn't just apply to the dogs she met while running around in the local parks. It also included the other dogs in the family, and while she didn't permanently live with any other dogs (until the last year of her life, but we'll get to that later),

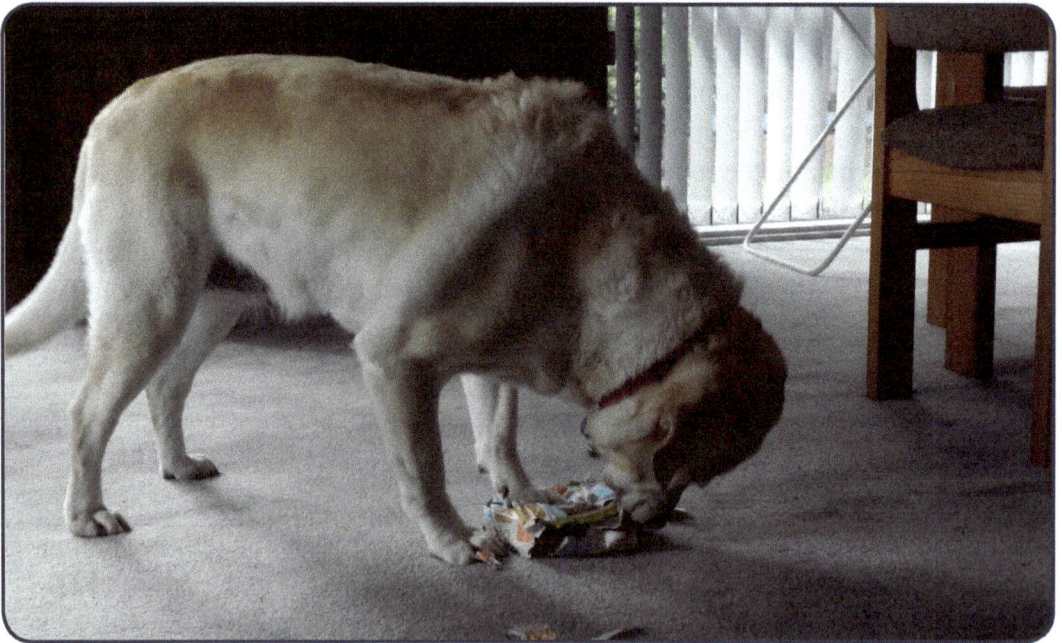

2013: Paris getting stuck in to opening her present on her 8th birthday.

there were several of whom she saw quite a lot. She loved and wanted to play with all of them, although not all of them felt quite as fondly for her.

The first two cousins she met were Eddie and Baylee, a Bichon Frise and Maltese Shih Tzu respectively, who both lived with my mum (and who would have therefore been present and accounted for during the Christmas chicken episodes already mentioned). Both being smaller, yappy dogs, they didn't immediately take to the imposition of a Labrador suddenly coming into their home and running around like she owned the place. They barked at her a lot, and occasionally she barked back, but all she wanted to do was play, and she would often slip and slide around on the hardwood floor trying to chase them.

It would be Paddy with whom she would be able to play properly. Paddy was a Kelpie belonging to my cousin who arrived in our family in late 2008, and he and Paris hit it off right away. He would always bark and go crazy every time he pulled up to our house in the back of my cousin's car because he knew he would be about to see Paris, who we jokingly called his girlfriend. Similarly whenever he sensed Paris coming up the driveway towards his place, using whatever doggy radar they have to sense the presence of other nearby dogs, he would get all excited and urinate everywhere.

Paddy wasn't just excitable, though. Typical of kelpies in general, he was an energetic dog, and we could always rely on him to wear Paris out—and lick her just about all over, requiring her to have a bath after he was gone. On the plus-side, though, when the two of them played, they really played. Paddy was the only dog I have ever seen match it with Paris in a game of tug-of-war; they went at it full-on just once that I can recall, in 2011 this was, and the battle was fierce and tightly contested. The only real loser that day was the rope they were playing with.

Also in 2011, another cousin entered the family. He was Harry, and he was a Shih Tzu belonged to Molly. He and Paris also got on well, and it was one of these early-days introductions between the two of them that caused the fabled 'pissathon' episode. Paris and I were visiting Molly in her new house for the first time, and Paris got so excited that she urinated inside for the first time in four years, and for the only time in her life when she wasn't sick. About a minute after that, Harry followed her lead and urinated in the kitchen, causing Molly to swear and me and my dad to laugh.

Harry and Paris would see a fair bit of each other on occasions over the following two years, but they would really get to bond when Molly and Harry came to live with us for a few weeks in 2013. My chief worry at this time was whether or not I would walk down the hallway only to step on a turd, or that Harry might get under my feet, not being used to living with a blind person. Paris learnt very quickly to get out of my way when I was coming towards her, and the only times she didn't move was when she was distracted by something else. Harry turned out to be a fine roomie for Paris, though, and there were no issues—until Paddy came to visit one day. Harry didn't like him at all, and when Paddy growled back, it set off a whole thing that necessitated the separation of the two dogs until Paddy had left.

In the last two years of Paris's life, she would make more friends through Sharlene, whom my dad began a relationship with in 2013. She had a couple of cats to whom Paris took an interest, but she never really got to play with them because every time Paris rocked up to the house, the cats would seemingly vanish, as if they had teleported to another postcode for the duration of the visit. Between Sharlene's three children, though, she met a few more doggy friends: Angel, AJ, Tyson; and towards the end, Irish Setter Jemima, the only one of these dogs that would be bigger than Paris, although that didn't stop Paris from bossing her around whenever they saw each other.

THE UNIVERSITY YEARS

As I said in an earlier chapter, it was Paris who enabled me to attend university for four years. I couldn't have done it without her—or if I had, it would have been ever so much more difficult. The campus I attended was fairly open, with buildings dotted in seemingly strange locations and in most cases, at strange angles to each other (that was how I imagined it in my mind, anyway). The openness of the main thoroughfare caused me to get lost a few times during the weeks before I got Paris, and on one occasion, I had to turn around and go home because the main path I used had been rendered impassable by tents and stalls for some event.

But although Paris made the campus much more accessible than it would have been otherwise, that didn't stop the two of us from having a few adventures during our time there. At the start of every semester, there would inevitably be at least one computer lab or lecture theatre in my schedule with which I wasn't familiar, and my dad would have to take me and Paris down to the campus to familiarise us with whatever route we needed to take to get there. Paris would thereafter remember the way, and all I would need to do was give her a figurative nudge in the right direction and she would do the rest.

At least, that was how it was supposed to work, and the majority of the time, it did, but a university campus is a dynamic environment, so you could never count on a route being as easy to negotiate as the day before. My favourite time of day to walk to class—any class, really—was first thing in the morning, because that was when things were nice and quiet, I wasn't being battered by sound all around me, and Paris and I didn't have to find our way through crowds of people, many of whom didn't look where they were going.

There were a few spots I dreaded negotiating, most of which were small doorways that easily bottlenecked after a lecture or tutorial. Those ones didn't really bother Paris so much, perhaps because she was small enough to fit through whatever gaps presented themselves to her—and never mind the poor bloke holding onto her. For me, it was partially being knocked around, and partially touching people in embarrassing ways, which gave me problems. On one notable occasion in 2009, on my way out of a corridor, I went to turn a doorknob but somehow grabbed a woman's breast instead. Don't laugh, I was too embarrassed to enjoy it!

Also in 2009, I started going to the gym at uni a couple of times a week—an exercise that lasted about eight months or so. I got sick halfway through the year which gave me an excuse not to go for a while, and I lost the rhythm of the thing after that. Paris and I would have to fight our way along a narrow but busy path to get to and from the gym, meaning that I was already a little buggered by the time we got there. I would then take Paris into the manager's office and tether her to the desk, with the manager's permission of course, while I went and did my work-out.

The only serious mishap Paris and I had on the uni campus is an incident which still lives on in infamy to this day. It happened in 2007, no more than two or three months after Paris graduated from training. She and I were coming out of a lecture theatre and were walking the path towards the exit, me being done for the day, when a slight miscommunication occurred. I thought Paris was walking me too far to the right, and I was concerned that she would walk me into some of the people there, so I kept nudging her towards the left.

Little did I realise that Paris was already doing what she'd been trained to do, and stick to the left-hand side of a wide path. Most seeing-eye dogs in Australia are trained to walk towards the left-hand side, consistent with the local road laws that say cars should drive on the left. That was what Paris did that day, not that I realized it; the thoroughfare was very wide and it was easy for a blind person to become disorientated while walking along it. So when Paris suddenly stopped walking, I got a little irritated with her, thinking that she must have been distracted by something happening to my right, and I urged her forward…

…And the next step I took, took me straight into a fountain. I suddenly dropped maybe a foot or a little more, not falling over but jarring myself badly enough to hobble me for several weeks. When I wasn't able to get out of the thankfully mostly dry fountain after twenty seconds or so, a confused Paris decided to jump down with me. Thank heavens for concerned passers-by, because I wouldn't have been able to get myself home under my own steam that day.

Most of the problems Paris and I would have while working together were caused by similar miscommunications between the two of us, although I can't recall any of the others being quite as painful as that one.

THAT WET DOG SMELL!

In the early years, Paris would only need a bath every month or two, although the period between baths would decrease as she got older. That schedule, however, didn't take extenuating circumstances into account; and quite a lot of the time, there were circumstances causing my dad and I to collar her and drag her to the bathroom sooner than that. It went like that because although she liked to swim, and she didn't seem to mind getting dirty, she had quite a low opinion of bath time.

If the weather was warm enough, it would be possible to bath Paris in a plastic tub in the back yard, although it would mean keeping her on the lead throughout so that she couldn't jump out and go running through the garden, getting herself all dirty again. Most of the time, though, we preferred to bath her in the bathroom, in the tub that she would have used throughout her life more than any of us humans did. Wherever we did it, though, it was a two-man operation, because Paris would make the process as difficult as she could.

The easiest way to get Paris in the bath would be to grab her by the collar and march her into the bathroom before the taps had been turned on; and even then, she would try to turn left into my bedroom instead of right into the bathroom. If she heard the water running into the tub, she would either try to hide, or move around a lot so that I couldn't catch her. I eventually figured out a system for tricking her when this happened; if I sat down in a seat and called to her, she would often come, thinking that I just wanted to pat her. Then once I had her, I would march her off to the bathroom.

The first few times, Paris would be very unwilling to jump into the tub; but eventually, once she was shut in the bathroom with me and my dad, she would recognize the hopelessness of her situation and dutifully save us a little trouble by jumping in. She would then wear a typically hangdog expression as we used a showerhead hooked up to the tap to soak her and then rub in the shampoo. For me, this was the most difficult part of the whole process, because Paris would lean against the other side of the bath, away from us, making it difficult to access all of her body. She also preferred to face the right, meaning that I always had her rear while my dad had her head, and she would be very unwilling to turn around when we needed her to.

Attempting to dry Paris was the most entertaining part of the process, and like the bath itself, it was definitely a two-man operation. Paris would be only too happy to jump out of the bath when we got out of the way and told her she could, shaking water in all directions and rolling and slipping around on the floor in her excitement. I would often have to hold her still while my dad dried her, or vice-versa, otherwise all that would happen was Paris would get tangled up in the towels. Later on, we got wise and dried her off as much as we could while she was still in the tub, although it didn't stop her shaking water all over us—I can only recall successfully ducking out of the line of fire once in nine years.

When we had done the best we could drying her, we would let Paris out of the bathroom. As soon as the door opened, she would disappear, rocketing through the house at top speed and doing massive figure-eight's through the lounge room and family room, and rolling around on the carpet and up against the lounge room wall. While my dad stayed back to clean up the bathroom (which would inevitably need to be cleaned up after the blonde bombshell that was Paris), I would follow after her, first to put her collar back on, and then to take her outside (after she'd calmed down a bit) so that I could brush her.

When she was wet was the best time to brush all that loose hair out of her, even if it meant that I'd have hairy palms for the rest of the day despite my best efforts to wash them, and I would have to put up with that infamous wet-dog smell that we all know and love. Paris became very well-known for dropping a lot of hair around the house and beyond, and I would like to say that brushing her when she was wet cut back on some of that hair, but the truth is I don't think it made much of a difference. She was like a hair machine that just kept producing; if we could have converted it into electricity, we could have disconnected from the grid for nine years.

A HORROR MOVIE

In mid-2010, my dad went overseas for about a month, leaving me and Paris running the show here. We handled things fine for the most part, although it was the only time I had to single-handedly give her a bath (which I somehow managed to do, although I probably made a real mess of it). Unfortunately there were a few things that we didn't manage so well, and one of these was the cause of a nightmare scenario about halfway through the four-week period.

Since I preferred to have a sighted person with me while free-running Paris, it meant that someone other than my dad would have to do it—something that happened rarely throughout her life. In this case, my cousin took us, and he brought Paddy as well, so that the two of them could run around together. That was good, but Paris had an unfortunate habit of eating the grass while out free-running (she sometimes did it at home as well), and while my dad would stop her as quickly as he could, my cousin made no real effort to do so other than to say, "Don't eat the grass, Paris, you're not a moo-moo-cow."

This left me to call to Paris, but most likely she was too far away to hear me—or far enough that she was able to pretend not to hear me. That was a regular thing for Paris to do on free-runs: Quite often when we were too lazy to bring the whistle or a bit of food to lure her back, Paris would be very unwilling to return to the car at the end of the run. She would either pretend not to hear the call for as long as she could get away with it, or she would return very slowly. It was considerably easier to put her back on the lead before leaving the park, if we were able to do so.

Anyway, on this particular occasion, I was worried that Paris might have eaten a lot of grass, something that would inevitably make her sick later on in the night. I dreaded the possibility that she might throw up while I was on my own; then I would have to clean it up, which would most likely require me to locate it with my hands (or if I was even less fortunate, my feet). And of course, later on that very night, waking me up a couple of hours after I had gone to sleep, came that horrible, deep belching sound from the corner of my room that could only mean one thing.

I scrambled out of bed, filled with dismay, to investigate the damage—and while she was still being sick, to make sure that she was throwing up on her bed rather than the carpet, and that she wouldn't try to lick it up afterwards. It was thoroughly disgusting, big and wet and chunky and positively reeking. Fortunately, it was all on Paris's bed, which meant that in theory, the clean-up operation should be much simpler.

I moved the bed out of the way, put down some towels for Paris to sleep on (just in

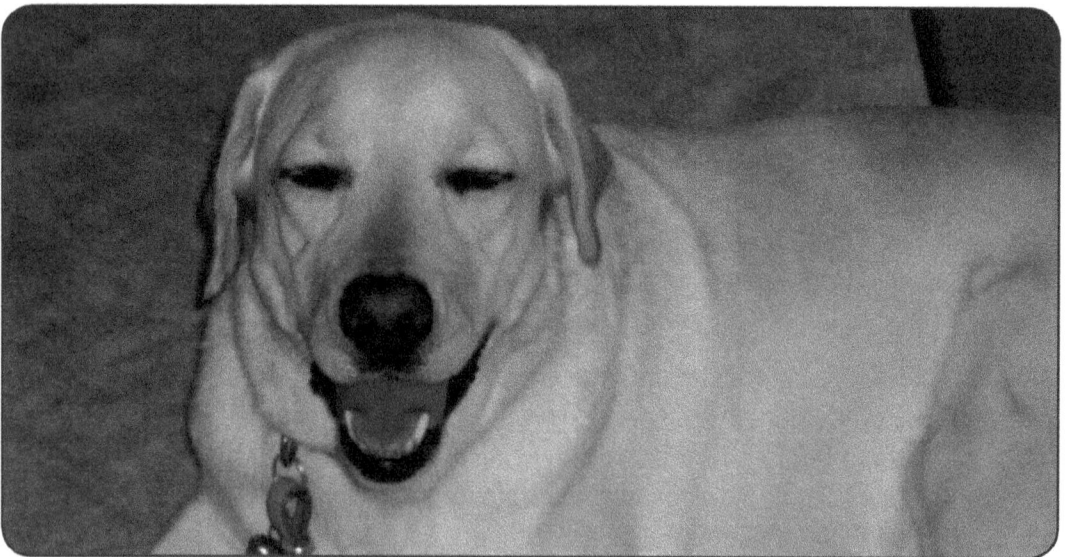

2012: Paris would always have a giggle at 'dad jokes'. I think she actually enjoyed a few of them sometimes!

case she threw up again), and then carried the bed out to the laundry. Because of the size of the bed, though, I had to hold it up over my head as I walked, so that I would be able to feel where I was going. And this was the point where my horror movie really began: About halfway there, I felt a cold wetness begin trickling down my hair from the top of my head. I cringed and moved faster; really it was all I could do not to wretch myself.

I eventually got the bed and its cover in the washing machine, but not after I scraped all the vomit off it and into the sink. I then ran the tap, foolishly thinking I could just wash the sick away, and in fact, I did manage to wash most of it away. Only when I put my hand back in the sink just to check, I found a whole handful of grass in there, much too much to wash away, so I put it in the bin instead. Needless to say, I wasn't particularly thrilled with my four-legged friend that night.

Also, needless to say, I went and had a very thorough shower before going back to bed.

FOLLOW-UP

It is standard SEDA policy to do follow-up training sessions with clients and their dogs, just to make sure everything's working fine and there are no issues. Paris and I received a handful of these visits during her working life, but the first of these didn't happen for at least two years after her graduation, though, because the trainer who had worked so much with Paris, Hadrian, apparently took Paris's papers with her when she left SEDA.

It didn't matter to us, though, because Paris and I were working quite fine without their assistance. In fact, each time that I got the call from the SEDA trainers letting me know that they wanted to do a follow-up, I would have to try to think of something to raise with them. Telling them I didn't need a follow-up wasn't an option because according to the handler agreement I'd signed back when I first applied, the visits were compulsory—I assume so that they can make sure the dog is still healthy, not being abused, and that it's working well enough to keep me safe.

Some of the follow-up visits were done by Trajan (who had first introduced me to the idea of getting a seeing-eye dog), while others were done by another trainer who we shall call Marcus. For me, the issue I raised with them more often than anything else was Paris's tendency to get distracted easily while out walking, and asking for ways that I could keep her mind on the job at hand. They helped me as best they could, and in fact I did learn a little from them, but ultimately no one was able to change that part of her personality. Marcus had ended up giving me a 'Gentle Leader', which was a loop that went over her nose that provided me with a way to keep her head forward when she tried to pull off to the side. I can tell you now that Paris did not enjoy wearing that thing, and would try to paw it off at every opportunity.

Most of the follow-up visits were done in the neighbourhood around my home where Paris and I did most of our walking. Usually we would do the walking and the trainer would watch from his car, following us in a way that would have creeped me out if I didn't know it was being done. On one such visit, Trajan kept pulling the car in front of us, stopping in front of us when we were halfway across the street, or pulling into a driveway just before we got to it. This was meant to teach Paris to stop and wait for the car, but Paris was confident in her abilities and actually managed to beat Trajan's car across the road on one of those occasions. Trajan advised me thereafter to slow her down while crossing streets so that in future, we would have time to react if a car showed up.

At least one session didn't take place in the local neighbourhood, though. I had considered asking to be shown how to take Paris on a bus or train, just in case I ever needed to do that, but I had just dropped out of university by that stage and had just decided to pursue writing as my career—I really couldn't foresee a time when we would need those skills. One place Paris and I did go with some frequency, though, was shopping centres, and we weren't very good at negotiating them (I would get very nervous because I couldn't tell if Paris was going the right way, and given her tendency to get distracted, my fears were justified).

So on one such session (2013, this would have been), Marcus took us to the nearest shopping centre for some training that included the two of us following him through a supermarket, and going up and down the escalators (dogs weren't normally trained to do that unless there were exceptional circumstances, because of the danger of losing their nails in the top or bottom of them). Paris did fine following Marcus, but maybe she just put on her best behaviour for him because she didn't repeat the feat months later; on that day, while following my dad, she decided to lead me directly between two women who were standing right next to each other.

As for going up and down the escalator, Paris did it perfectly during training, and she was so proud of herself that the next time we did it, she got all excited and tried to go running up the escalator. When I tried to pull her back, she slipped and fell, not hurting herself that time (thankfully), but according to Marcus, it could have happened, and that in future I would have to restrain her without pulling her. We never had that problem again, but weeks later when I was with my dad, we tried it again and there was another problem, this one not immediately obvious.

Later in the evening, Paris kept licking one of her front paws, and the following day, she was limping on it. The day after that (a Monday), the limp was even worse, so we took her to the vet. To this day, I'm not entirely sure what was wrong with that paw, and I still have no proof that it was caused by the escalator. Nevertheless, I never took her on another one after that day, and most fortunately, it was easily fixed. The vet gave her an injection and told us to keep her off it as much as possible for a week or so, but within a few hours of that, Paris seemed to be back to her normal self, and the limp never returned.

THE SUMMER DOGGY

Paris definitely preferred the cooler temperatures over the warmer ones. When summer time came around, and particularly on those really hot days where the temperature got into the high-30s and 40s, she would really struggle. She would be malting like no one's business, panting whenever she walked anywhere or did anything, drank lots more water, and would lie down and sleep in the laundry where the non-carpeted floor meant that it was a tad cooler. It also meant that when I brushed her during those times, quite apart from filling the brush with hair, I would occasionally get electric shocks off her.

We did try to find ways to make it more comfortable for her. My dad would occasionally take her outside and turn the hose on her, but for some strange reason, Paris didn't particularly enjoy that any more than she enjoyed bath times. We had an inflatable kiddie pool that we blew up for Paris (and to soak our own feet in as well), which Paris would step in and out of from time to time, and occasionally take a drink out of it. We also gave her blocks of ice from the freezer to chew on, just to cool her down a little on the inside, but the silly dog would take them and play with them on the carpet, making a mess everywhere.

She didn't get a lot of opportunities to go swimming, mainly because of the hassle it meant for us. In the early days when we took her free-running in a park that had a creek, she would jump in and get herself incredibly dirty, and then I would have to put up with her making me all wet and dirty on the car ride home (more about that in the next chapter).

She did manage to go swimming in a full-sized swimming pool only a couple of times (once at my mum's place, and once at a friend's house on a 40-degree day), and both times, she filled the pools up with hair and was forbidden from any future swimming. Years later when she returned to that friend's house for a pool party, she got to lie at the side of the pool and dip her paws in, but was prevented by her leash from getting any closer. Poor Paris whined a little that night, but sadly, the rules were established.

One place where she was allowed to go swimming, though, was the beach. For a long time, we hadn't taken her there, mainly because we ourselves didn't like it, but in February of 2012, my dad and I decided to give it a go. It didn't really go well; Paris ran into the water, made a choking sound that caused us both to laugh, and then came running back out again. She went in a second time but after that, she preferred to stay with us—only now, she was soaking and giving off that notorious wet dog smell. We never took her back there, figuring that it would be much easier to stick to the tools we had at home—namely the kiddy pool and the hose.

PARIS ON WHEELS

Given that she was a seeing-eye dog, Paris and I probably ended up getting driven places more often than we walked there. When I first got Paris, SEDA showed me the proper way to take her in a car: It would involve me getting in the front seat (the passenger's side, obviously), putting one leg in, and then giving Paris room to jump in before putting my other leg in. Then while we were driving, she would be on the floor in the front seat between my legs.

In the early days, we would always follow this procedure, and even later on we sometimes stuck to it, depending on who was driving me and how many other people were in the car with us. It always meant putting the seat back all the way so that there would be room for the doggy, and then I would often have to put the window down so that she could stick her nose out for fresh air. If she wasn't interested in that, she would usually eventually lie down with her head in my lap, in a position that must not have been very comfortable, but she didn't seem to mind it.

One time that we would always drive Paris rather than walk was when we took her for free-runs, and I did not enjoy the ride back with Paris in the front seat with me. If I was lucky, she would only be panting and dribbling all over me (which was fine if I were wearing pants, not so good if I were wearing shorts). If I were unlucky, she would also be wet and dirty; this would happen if she jumped in the creek, or more often if she ran through a puddle of mud (and on at least one occasion that I

2013: Paris about to take revenge and give me a big lick on the nose and yep, she got me.

can recall, stopped and lay down in it). We kept a towel in the back of the car to deal with her for when this happened, but it would never be enough to make the ride back home bearable.

More often in the latter years (from 2012 onwards), Paris would sit in the back seat rather than the front. It was my dad's initiative, which I initially opposed simply because that wasn't how I'd been taught to do it, but in the end I was brought around by the sheer logic of it: It was just easier that way. He started doing it after he retired and would go and buy a copy of the day's newspaper, putting Paris in the back seat so that she could have a little car ride. The first couple of times she sat in the back when I was in the car with her were long drives (one a wine tasting for my 25th birthday, and one a three-day holiday up at the Victoria-New South Wales border— part of the purpose of the latter had been to shoot a promotional video for my first book, 'The Seventh Sorcerer'), and apart from her once barking at a man who came to the window, it proved to be so much easier than having a female dog between my legs.

I ended up quite enjoying having Paris in the back seat, because not only did I have more space for my legs, but I still got to pat her by leaning back between the seats (to which Paris would inevitably lick my probing hand). When Alysha was also in the car, she thoroughly enjoyed sharing the back seat with Paris—you could be sure to hear the cries of "Doggydoggydoggydoggydoggy" as soon as she got in and Paris greeted her.

The only time it wasn't so fun was in 2015 when we were taking Paris to a kennel for the night (it was a wedding up in the mountains where we would be staying overnight, and taking Paris was impractical). It wasn't fun that time because Alysha and I were both in the back seat with Paris; we'd thought, before we did it, that there would be enough room for the three of us, but we were sorely mistaken. We under-estimated just how much space Paris took up; she sat between us, balanced precariously with her front legs on the floor (because there wasn't enough room on the seat for all four legs), gazing between the two seats as though to say to my dad, "Get me out of here." And when she wasn't in that position, one or more of her legs would be digging into my right thigh, and I would be the one not enjoying myself.

WINNING AND LOSING

I would like to take this chapter to tell a couple of stories which don't exactly focus on Paris, but which she managed to play a role in. In the first story, it was her presence which caused me to win; while in the second, it was her presence which caused me to lose. The first happened in winter 2011 while the second happened roughly six months later.

2012: Paris and me in Corowa enjoying a long weekend away from home.

In July or August of 2011, my dad and I went to a sports social lunch put on by a local radio station in Melbourne. We had been meaning to do it earlier but the lunches always happened on Friday afternoon, so it couldn't be done until after my dad retired. At one point in the proceedings, they played a game called 'sit down if you…', in which the last person standing won a prize.

I was one of the last few people standing, so my dad took me out the front, and I brought Paris out with me. I was quickly eliminated after that when the person running the game said, "sit down if you have a seeing-eye dog", and when people started saying, "you can't do that", he jokingly claimed, "I didn't see the dog!" I went and sat back down, but then the game ended in a tie, so without a clear winner, people started calling out, "Give it to the dog," which by extension meant me. So thanks to Paris, I won a crappy dash-cam and a mouse pad which I never used. Cheers!

I got a bit of a kick out of that, but I wasn't feeling so cheerful months later— although admittedly I was laughing a lot, even though I ended up losing humiliatingly. It was after dinner at my mum's place when we (me, my mum, my step dad whose name also happened to be Stephen, my sister Molly and my brother Zac) started a games night on the Nintendo Wii. We had two games of Wii bowling, and I smashed the competition in the first game with six strikes. I only needed to be pointed in the right direction and then I could deliver these perfect bowls which were almost identical each time. At least, that's how it was before I lost my concentration.

The second game got off to an average start for me (I didn't pull away from the pack like I did in the first), but then on my third turn, when I went to bowl, I accidentally smacked Paris in the head with the controller. Everyone started laughing, and Paris quickly got out of my way (she wasn't hurt), and on the TV screen, the ball I'd just bowled went straight into the gutter. The game continued after that, but my concentration was gone, and there were no further strikes—I went down in a big way. I gave Paris a good long pat after that and told her that she'd done a good job getting involved in the game.

A THOUSAND MILES APART

I mentioned a couple of chapters ago that Paris went to stay overnight at a kennel in 2015. That was the only time that ever happened, and it was one of only four times since Paris first arrived at my house that she and I were apart at night time (not counting a couple of times I was in hospital in 2015, but that's for later). The other three times were when I went overseas (once to New Zealand and twice to Bali), and in all three cases, Paris didn't come with me because it just seemed like more trouble than it would be worth.

When I went to New Zealand, it was less than a year after I first got Paris, and I was a little uneasy about being away from her. She remained at home, looked after by Alysha while my dad was also on holidays in Queensland, and then by him when he returned. They handled her fine, although on one afternoon, Alysha went all over the house looking for Paris, but the dog never answered her call until hours later when, while on her way to the bathroom, Alysha overheard a thumping sound that turned out to be Paris wagging her tail from under my dad's bed, where she had been all along.

The first time I went to Bali was in early February of 2009, and it was a family holiday—that is to say, my dad and Alysha came with me. Paris was left with my cousin, who was initially going to house-sit for us, but in the end decided to take Paris back to his place for most of the duration because our house didn't have air conditioning, and the weather in Melbourne at that time was brutally hot (Black Saturday was two days after we left). It wasn't just better for my cousin though; Paris was undoubtedly more comfortable at his place, plus she got to spend close to a week with Paddy—something she definitely would have enjoyed.

The second time I went to Bali was four years later, and this time it was just me and

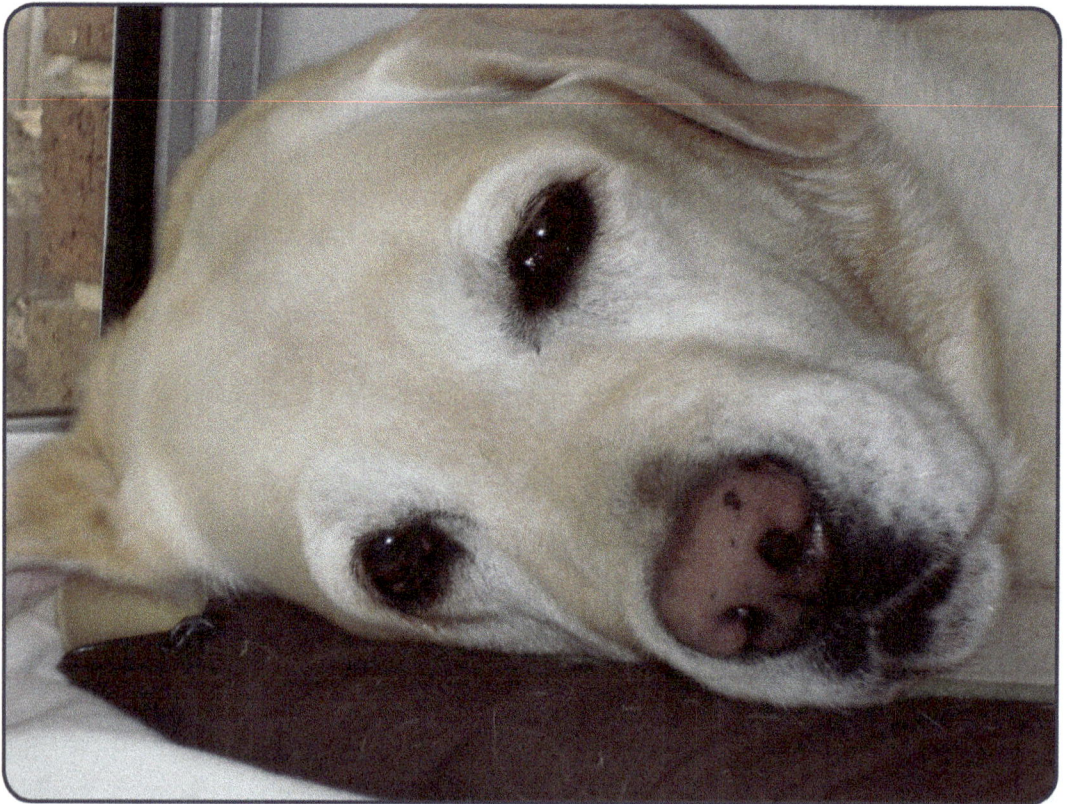

2008: Paris snuggles down in her bed in my room.

my dad going. Molly was commissioned to house-sit this time, which meant that she was also commissioned to dog-sit Paris. They didn't have any major issues; in fact, it gave them time to really bond. They went for walks every evening (the weather was still good at that time), and quite likely Paris was given greater liberty to eat foods that she normally wouldn't be allowed to eat. To top it off, Harry stayed over as well, so Paris had a week-long playmate.

Molly was also exposed to a couple of other quirks that came with Paris, which I had learnt about years earlier. One night, Paris farted in the bedroom, making it virtually uninhabitable for quite a while due to the overpowering stench. Another night, while they were both in and on their respective beds, Paris let loose an almighty bark without any warning, making Molly jump out of her skin—not unlike the ones that I was subjected to way back when Paris and I were living in the SEDA house.

ROOMIES

Earlier in the story, I described the various dogs with which Paris had regular contact over her life, but I left one dog out—perhaps the one that would ultimately be her best friend over all. His name was JJ, a Pomeranian-Chihuahua cross who was a rescue dog from the RSPCA and adopted by my dad's partner Sharlene in mid-2014. He was a strange little dog, a bit shy and unsociable, but thanks mainly to the smart way that we introduced the two of them, he and Paris would quickly become very good mates.

Before she brought him home, we took Paris down to the kennel where JJ was being kept so that they could meet, keeping Paris on her lead so that she couldn't bounce around and intimidate the little dog. It was decided that it would be better to do the introduction there rather than at home, where Paris was bound to be territorial, growling and barking and scaring JJ so much that he would never want to return. It was a tactic that we had used in similar situations where we would need to introduce Paris to a dog with which we anticipated she would have a lot of contact, and it had worked well in the past.

Over the following nine months or so, Paris and JJ would spend a good amount of time together, whether they were playing together (usually one chasing the other, as JJ was too small to play tug-of-war with Paris), or napping in various locations around the house. Luckily for JJ, Paris was aging by this time and had slowed down somewhat; she wouldn't be much interested in playing tug-of-war at all for too much longer.

In the first half of 2015, Sharlene moved in and brought JJ with her, so that for the first time since becoming my seeing-eye dog, Paris had a full-time roomy. It turned

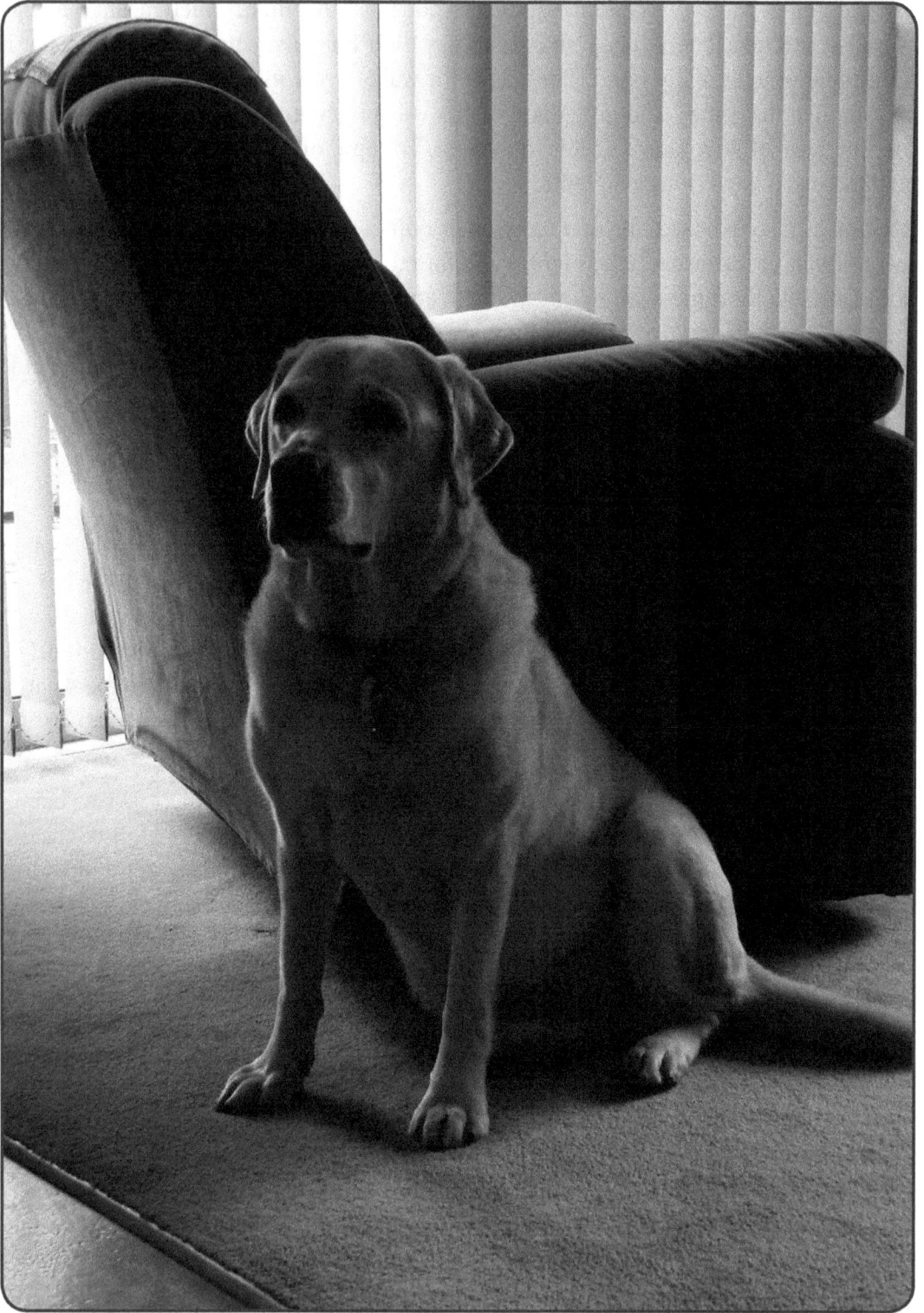

Paris on her 8th birtrhday taking great interest in what's happening in the kitchen.

out not to be a problem for either of them; in fact, they quickly settled into a routine. Or more accurately, JJ settled into Paris's routine, and Paris merely adapted to his presence. For instance, when I went to see my personal trainer twice a week, instead of just Paris sitting up in the back of the car, going for a free-run in the nearby park while I was working out, now both dogs went for a run together.

I was particularly amused by the way they went about dinner. They would almost always eat at the same time, Paris in the laundry and JJ in the garage, with a closed door separating the two of them so that Paris wouldn't go for JJ's food once she was done with her own. After she'd finished eating (well before JJ most of the time), she and I would go out to the garage for the daily brush, which became more difficult for me because not only did I have to hold her in place so that she wouldn't get up and investigate JJ's food, but she would constantly turn her head to look at it, which made the brushing itself more difficult.

Then when JJ was finished eating, he would wander up the driveway to have a piss somewhere, and Paris would lick up whatever he left behind. In the early days, JJ would eat some of his dinner and wander away, only to return to finish it or eat a little more. Once he got used to Paris, though, he quickly learnt that if he didn't eat all of it immediately, there wouldn't be any left for him later. Sometimes I would have to take Paris inside because JJ was taking a particularly long time finishing his dinner, but if the back door was open at the time (as it usually was when the weather was warm), Paris would go through it and through the back of the garage—a sneaky trick that would come close to working.

It wasn't her only sneaky trick to get JJ's food either. One night when it was left up to me and Alysha to feed both dogs, we put a lot of work into keeping the two of them separate so that JJ could eat his dinner. But sadly, nothing we tried worked because JJ, perhaps put off by me giving him dinner instead of Sharlene or my dad, didn't want to eat it. Then while Alysha was blocking the door, Paris managed to squeeze past her without her noticing and go for JJ's dinner; and when I heard the eating sounds, I thought it was JJ. So the little doggie missed out, but since he chose not to eat it when he had the chance, I don't have a lot of sympathy for him.

As for Paris, well let's just say she knew how to work the system.

THE SUPPORTIVE DOGGY

Earlier in the book, I explained how Paris and I bonded more during a time of personal stress for me. In that case, it was mostly by my initiative; that is to say, I would find Paris and then the two of us would play, or I would give her a nice, big cuddle, or so on. But Paris's companionship went deeper than just being a furry friend when you wanted one; she often had a good sense of when someone was in some sort of distress, and she would try to lend her support in her own way.

I learnt this at some stage in the first few years (I can't remember exactly when it was) when I got really upset by the family fighting around me, and Paris immediately came and pressed her head against my side to lend me strength—at least that's how it felt at the time.

I also learnt it twice in 2015 when I broke my arms; my left arm in July, and my right one in December. The first break was a freakish accident in my own home, and fortunately Paris knew better than to come too close to me while I was on the floor in agony—she probably would have hurt me. She did, however, wet-nose me as I was being assisted onto a stretcher, as if to show me her concern and to ask me what was going on.

As for the second break, it involved falling down a couple of steps and landing on my arm (after a few drinks), and Paris was right beside me at the time. Rather than walk around inquisitively as she might have done under normal circumstances, Paris simply lay down beside me on the ground while we waited for the ambulance to arrive.

And that support didn't only stretch to me, her master; it would extend to anyone close to her who needed it. For instance, Alysha broke her leg in mid-2010 and was hobbled for some time. When she had to walk up the hallway in our house, moving much more slowly than usual, Paris walked alongside her, keeping the same slow pace, as if to say that it was okay to go slowly. She did the same thing for me two years later when I hurt my leg (ironically while out walking with her).

SIGNS OF AGING

Paris began to show signs that she was really getting on in years in the second half of 2014, but we were given a warning a little earlier than that by the presence of a couple of lipomas on her body. Alysha was the first to notice them, and terrified that they might be cancerous, demanded that we take Paris to the vet to have them checked. That was one of only two times prior to the last month of her life that Paris went to the vet for anything other than an annual check-up—the other time being that escalator incident I mentioned earlier. The vet told us that they were harmless little lumps and that they were common in aging dogs, but that was all the proof we needed that despite her general good health, Paris was no longer the playful puppy she once was.

Around her ninth birthday (October the 1st, 2014), her behaviour also began to change. It was around that time that she tended to spend more time sleeping than anything else, although she was still fit when it came to working (for a while in late 2014 and early 2015, she and I walked up and down a hill near home to improve my fitness). When it came to playing, she tended to have considerably less energy than she did as a pup. She would still play tug-of-war as hard as ever, but she would only have enough energy for one or two rounds before she'd had enough. Additionally, she would be much less interested in running and fetching something than she had once been.

She would still enjoy free-runs, but by this time they weren't so much free-runs as they were free-walks. Instead of getting exercise, she would mostly gallivant through the grass, sniffing and snuffling at everything in sight. Only when there were other dogs around would she get livelier, and even then it wasn't quite as much as it used to be. The only thing that didn't change was her reluctance to get back in the car once the free-run had ended.

The part of this that bothered me the most, however, was how she slept. For reasons I couldn't understand at the time, Paris had become totally uninterested in sleeping on her bed in my room, as she had been doing since the beginning, preferring instead to sleep in the family room (or under my dad's bed if she could get away with it). After some consideration, I had let her do this, although it didn't take long for me to miss her company—even just her rolling over or snuffling in the night.

We joked at the time that these changes were a doggy version of menopause, and maybe it really was something like that. Looking back on it now, though, I think maybe we all had our heads in the sand to some degree. I knew that Paris was nine years old, and I knew that she was getting older, but I still believed that she probably had at least two more years of working life ahead of her, and maybe another two years of retirement after that. I turned out to be awfully mistaken.

PARIS, THE GRUMP

When I broke my left arm in mid-2015, it meant that I was unable to work Paris for several months. Then shortly after I did start working her again, I broke my right arm, which slowed me down for a few more weeks. (This discrepancy exists because Paris was only trained to walk on my left side.) What this meant, although we didn't know it at the time, was that Paris went into a sort of unofficial retirement in July of 2015. She would work in harness again a few more times in late 2015 and early 2016, but those times would be negligible—a sort of encore, if you will.

It was in the second half of 2015 that another change in behaviour began to effect Paris, and this definitely worried us at the time—although again, if we'd known how little time Paris had left, we probably would have worried less). There were a few incidents with Paris and other dogs—little dogs, to be more accurate. These little dogs would be yappy and aggressive towards her, but where in the past Paris would just ignore them (or continue trying to play with them), now she growled back at them and tried to grab the back of their necks with her teeth—not so much to hurt them, but more to dominate them.

The first time it happened was on Jemima's first birthday (the Irish setter mentioned earlier in the book), when another smaller dog arrived at the party, and he and Paris quickly got off on the wrong foot. After the incident that followed, the small dog and its owners quickly left the party—he wasn't hurt, but everyone was in shock. Paris was put back on her lead for the remainder of the night. To her credit, she quickly realized that she'd done something naughty, and shame-facedly stuck by my side after that.

Less than two months later, it happened again, and this one was even more shocking. It was another party setting, though this time it was in a public park. One moment, Paris was lying beside me, tethered to the leg of the table I was sitting at; in the next, she had bolted away, so hard and fast that she busted right out of her collar, breaking the clasp and requiring me to buy her a new one. When I heard growling behind me, I didn't think for a moment that it could be Paris, because she was tied up right

2014: Paris at her best, bright eyed and grinning from ear to ear.

beside me, but then I put my hand down to make sure of that, and there was no dog to be found.

What had happened was Paris must have made eye contact with a little yappy dog that was being walked nearby by a stranger. She had gone after it and grabbed it, taking the woman walking it by surprise and requiring some of the people with us to grab her and haul her back to me. The strange woman reassured me that her dog had been the aggressor, but I'd still been most concerned about this recent trend in Paris's behaviour, and not just because it meant that I had to hold onto her for the rest of the night, her collar now being totally ineffective.

There had been another incident of this happening while free-running, but this had been while I was at the gym. The trend worried me, and I seriously considered contacting SEDA to ask them if there was anything I could do about it, but I talked myself out of making the call. This was partially because there were no more incidents following that one at the park (which had been in November 2015), and because I didn't want SEDA to force me to retire her on those grounds. I still wanted to keep Paris in her job for another year or so, giving her ten full years of work life, so I took a chance that Paris would stop behaving like this.

As it was, SEDA had been in touch with me shortly following the break of my right arm, wanting to do a follow-up session. Because of the break, I was able to put it off until the first week of March in 2016, but the way Paris worked that day under Trajan's supervision made it clear that while she was still capable of working, we would have to look at retirement again in six months or so. It was clear that Paris had become very tired by the end of the walk, but we put that down to the weather conditions on the day (it was already over 30 degrees at ten o'clock in the morning when we stepped outside), but we didn't really consider that it was a result of Paris's poor health instead.

That follow-up session in the first week of March, 2016, was the last time Paris ever worked.

THE HOME STRAIGHT

Wednesday, 16th March 2016, was one of the worst days of my entire life. It was the day that Paris was diagnosed with anaemia and suspected cancer, and it became very clear to us all that her days were numbered. It began late the previous week when we started noticing that Paris wasn't well; she was a lot more lethargic than usual, and she was going off her food. We had to wait until Tuesday to take her to the vet because the Monday had been a public holiday, and they immediately agreed that

2016: Paris and JJ huffing and puffing after a run at the park.

there was something wrong. They performed a blood test and would let us know the results the following day.

We knew it was bad before we got the call though, not just from her behaviour around the house but also JJ's manner; he could tell that something was wrong too. At one point on that Wednesday morning, he and Paris nosed each other, as if he were telling her that he'd be with her whatever happened, or just to lend her some of his strength. Or maybe it was his way of telling her goodbye, because once we had the full picture of what was going on inside Paris's body, it was clear that if something wasn't done, she would be dead by the end of the week.

The blood tests showed that she had cancer of the liver and spleen coupled with severe anaemia, but a more thorough scan would be required to get the full gist of what was happening. Paris had that done at a more specialized clinic, whereas everything else up to this point had been done by the vet around the corner from our home. What we learnt by four o'clock that afternoon was that the cancer was all through her liver and spleen, and that while it would be possible to remove the spleen, extending her life a little, there was nothing they could do for the liver. They also gave her a blood transfusion while she was there so that she would have the strength to survive the surgery.

We were all in various states of shock when we went to pick Paris up from the clinic and take her back to the local vet where she would have the operation. Molly and Alysha had both been crying on the phone that day, and my dad was talking incessantly about the things we were driving past on the way to the clinic, as though trying to keep his mind busy so that he wouldn't break down. As for me, I was holding Paris's lead in my lap during the drive, and just holding it was forcing me to recall all the good times I'd ever had with Paris, as I started to come to terms with the fact that she wasn't going to be around much longer.

My composure broke when I was reunited with Paris at the clinic. While my dad and Sharlene went to look at the scans (to see the tumors for themselves), Paris and I were left alone on the floor in the middle of the waiting room. I tried to order her to sit down, not wanting her to use any more energy than she had to, and maybe she started to do so, but then she just allowed herself to slide onto her belly with a little grunt.

Perhaps her head was a little dizzy from the recent blood transfusion, or maybe she was in pain; either way, she kept letting out these quiet little whines that were barely audible, but just loud enough for me to hear. They broke my heart and caused me to finally break down, as I'd needed to do most of the day, and I spent the time before my dad and Sharlene returned reassuring Paris (or myself) that it was going to be okay.

We took an exhausted Paris back to the vet and had to let our hearts break a little more when we left her there for the night. The hardest part was her watching us leaving, wanting to come with us—because after all the moving around during the day, all Paris wanted to do was go home and rest. We then spent the rest of that night anxiously waiting to hear from the vet; and finally, when I'd just about given up hope that we would hear anything that night, they called and let us know that the surgery had gone well and Paris was resting comfortably.

We brought her home the next morning, and she was very happy to be there. She slept most of that Thursday afternoon, but then she got up as the pain from the surgery set in, and she was unable to settle down all through the night and into the next morning. Both Molly and Alysha got to see Paris during this time; and in Molly's case, when Paris came around the corner and saw her walking through the front door, she (Paris) actually cried, causing Molly to cry again.

We were all filled with all kinds of emotions, the chief of which was obviously deep sadness, but there was also some guilt mixed in. We had known for some time that Paris was a little off, and we hadn't done anything about it. Paris herself had done a good job of hiding any pain she might have been feeling, at least right up until the week the diagnosis came in. It was as if she were trying to stay strong for me; such behaviour fit with how she had always wanted to make me happy and proud of her while working. Sadly, it meant that by the time we knew there was a serious problem, it was far too late to do much about it.

Over the following couple of weeks, Paris actually recovered somewhat. It wasn't a full recovery; she was still in a small amount of pain, and her energy levels were low, but some of the old dogginess came back into her. The trouble we had with her regarded her food and her medication; she quickly learnt that she didn't like the tablets she had been proscribed, and we had to get creative to get her to swallow them. Even putting them in the middle of succulent meat, the kind she had never been allowed to eat before now, didn't do the trick, because she would just swallow the meat and somehow manage to spit the tablet out.

2014: Paris at work with me on the streets.

We became much more relaxed with Paris in those weeks, given that it was so late in the game for her. It didn't seem like there was any need to enforce the rules that SEDA had laid out for her, especially given that she was now officially retired from working. I made the decision on that fateful Wednesday as soon as I found out that she had cancer, and we were sure to let Trajan know what was going on—which was bitterly ironic, given that we had been talking about her retirement with him just two weeks earlier.

Paris stayed reasonably well just long enough for us to get our hopes up that she might live a little longer. One thing we didn't know about her cancer was exactly how malignant it was or wasn't; the tumors still on her liver could have been benign, and maybe they wouldn't have spread through her body too quickly. As it was, it was the anaemia, rather than the cancer, that got her in the end. It returned with a vengeance around the end of March, slowing her right down and once again putting her off her food.

It was around this time that my dad broached, on a couple of separate occasions, the possibility that I might have to consider putting Paris to sleep. He needn't have worried about making me uncomfortable with the topic, though, because it was something I had been contemplating ever since I first learnt of her illness. I wasn't in any hurry to make such a devastating call, but at the same time, I knew that I would rather do that than allow her to die a slow and painful death, as it would have been if we had given the cancer time to spread all through her.

In the first week of April, I considered that it would probably need to be done the following week, because of the downward spiral that seemed to have taken hold of Paris by this time. I was worried that she could die on her own very soon, and I was utterly horrified by the thought of it happening when I wasn't around to say a final goodbye—and on a more unpleasant note, the thought of finding her lifeless body also horrified me somewhat. My dad talked me out of it, mainly because it was his 60th birthday on the 16th of April, and none of us really wanted to ruin what should have been a happy occasion with something so sad.

On the 10th of April, we took Paris down to Molly's house for a visit, also giving her a chance to see Harry again for what would probably be the last time. Paris hadn't been all that interested in going; she slept almost the entire time we were there, plus both car rides, but she did manage to find the strength to jump up into the back seat on both occasions. That was an improvement on how she had been when going to the vet a month earlier, when we'd had to pick her up and help her into the back seat. Paris may not have appreciated that outing, but I don't regret taking her, because it turned out that it was the last time Paris left her home until the very end.

FLY WITH THE ANGELS, PARIS

In the last few days of her life, Paris was barely able to move, and on more than one occasion had to be carried places. She went almost completely off her food; no one else was able to get her to eat anything, and only I was able to get her to gobble some pieces of meat out of my hand (it was pretty disgusting, but I was just happy that she got a little food into her). When she went to the toilet, she was too weak to even stand up, and could only lie on the grass and let her stools slide out of her.

On the day before her death, I went out for most of the afternoon, but before I left, my dad helped Paris into my bedroom so that she could lie on her bed. When I returned later that night, I learnt that she hadn't moved all day, and my dad said there was a possibility that she might not live through the night. The thought terrified me, causing me to stay up all night with Paris, but that wasn't the only reason why I stayed up with her: I knew myself that it was the last night of her life. She was just so weak and no longer had any quality of life. It would have been cruel to drag this out any longer.

I spent much of the night sitting beside Paris's bed, patting her periodically and listening to the sound of her rapid breathing, terrified that it might change or stop altogether. We had brought some of her food in, just in case she was hungry, but Paris never touched it. There was also a bowl of water for her but she was too weak to get up on her front legs enough to drink out of it, unless I brought it right up to her mouth, which I occasionally did. Sometimes I just dipped my hand in the water and then put it against her mouth, and she would be happy enough to lick all the moisture

2016: Paris displays signs of fatigue at the park.

off it. I know she appreciated me being there with her because whenever I put my hand near her tail, she would wag it a bit; it was a weak wag, but it was there.

Paris did manage to get up once in the night, though, taking me by surprise. The first time was around midnight; she made it almost all the way to my bedroom door and then collapsed, unable to go any further. The reason why she got up was obvious; she needed to go to the toilet. I was eventually able to get her up and help her back onto her bed, but what came out of her onto my carpet was one hundred percent liquid, and as I was to learn in the morning when my dad got a look at it, it was tinged with blood.

Knowing that she was now bleeding internally on top of everything else only confirmed what I already knew: This couldn't go on any longer. It wasn't just Paris suffering now. Everyone around her was suffering as well, watching her deteriorate in this way. So after we'd had our breakfast, my dad helped Paris get on her feet and then carried her outside so that she could spend her last morning in the sunshine. I told him that it was time, and then while I had a nap in the morning, exhausted from being up all night, he called the vet and asked if they could come around today and euthanise her at our place. We wanted to do it here because this was Paris's home, and she deserved to go to sleep somewhere she would be comfortable.

The appointment was set for two o'clock that afternoon, and the call went out, letting everyone know that it was happening that afternoon. Sharlene immediately dropped everything at work and came home so that she could be with my dad. Alysha and Molly both had much the same tearful reaction when they were told: "I'm not

2016: JJ never got too far away from Paris at the park and this day, he didn't leave her side.

ready." I couldn't blame them, and I felt terrible for being the one who made the call, but I had to remind myself that however hard this was, it was the right thing to do. Both of them came around to visit Paris one last time, but while Molly chose to stay, Alysha couldn't bear to be present when it happened, and so she left shortly before the vet arrived—right on time.

When the doorbell rang, Paris tried to bark her disapproval that someone would dare enter her territory, as she had been doing for most of her time with us. It was a heart-breakingly weak bark, though, and she only managed three soft "woofs" before giving up. The same vet who had operated on her weeks earlier came in and set up beside Paris, where she was lying on her bed in the centre of the family room. We had put her there so that we could all be around her at the end: Me, Molly, my dad, Sharlene, and even JJ—although JJ didn't want to get close to Paris now, perhaps sensing that something big and bad was about to happen.

The feeling was so surreal for me as the vet prepped Paris, because I knew what was about to happen, and I also knew that it wasn't too late to call the whole thing off. Part of me wanted to do that so badly, and it took all the strength I had not to give in to the temptation. When the vet was ready, we were all given one last chance to say goodbye to her, and I leaned over her and gave her a cuddle, now fighting back tears—I hadn't cried since that fateful day four weeks ago when the diagnosis came in. I wished that Paris could have given me some sort of sign then, but she just lay there—she was too weak to do anything else.

I didn't let go of Paris after that, and my hand was still on her back when the vet quietly said, "She's gone." I hadn't felt anything; there was no final shudder or anything. Paris simply stopped breathing, and that was it. The floodgates opened then, and I'll never forget Molly's immediate cries of "No, bring her back!" I'll also never forget that light-headed feeling that swept over me in that moment as it hit home that Paris was really, truly, gone.

The vet packed up and took Paris away after that so that she could be cremated, and since she was a seeing-eye dog, they would give us her ashes in a nice box free of charge. As he was carrying her out, the vet put a sheet over Paris so that we wouldn't have to look at her, but Molly made him pull it back, uncovering her head, so that it looked like she were just sleeping. My dad took my hand and put it on Paris's lifeless head just before she was taken away; I appreciated it, but maybe I would have been better off not feeling her then.

The official time of death was 2:10pm on Wednesday, 13th April, 2016.

FOREVER PARISIAN

It took a good couple of weeks for me to get past grieving for Paris, and the first few days were the worst. The night after her death, after I'd had my dinner, I automatically turned to go into the laundry, where I normally fed her, before remembering that she was no longer with us; I had to hurry to my bedroom so that I could break down again in privacy.

Also in the first couple of days after her death, I kept sensing things that seemed to be like Paris, such as imagining that I could feel dog hair floating against my face. In the hours after her death, I also imagined that I heard sounds that were like her—the sound of her paws hitting the carpet, and a snuffling sound that reminded me very much of Paris. To this day, I don't know what actually made those sounds.

My favourite, though, took place two days later in the car after a session with my personal trainer, which up until then, Paris had come along for. When my dad turned the radio on, the first words spoken by the announcer were, "G'day Paris". Someone by the name of Paris had called up the station, but I took the timing and the sheer coincidence of it as a sign that Paris was still with us in spirit, perhaps riding along in the backseat with JJ.

As for JJ, he was not quite right for a while after Paris's death. He kept looking around for her, and it may have taken him several days to realise that she wasn't coming back. He went through his own form of grieving which included not wanting to change the routine that he'd gotten used to, the one that revolved around Paris. It was with some effort that my dad and Sharlene got him to eat in the kitchen instead of the garage, which was no longer necessary now that we didn't have to keep Paris away from his dinner.

We heard very little from SEDA after Paris was gone. Trajan only came around once to collect her harness, and his visit didn't go

2016: Paris hiding under the table for the last time.

over too well with the family. We got a sense that he didn't have a lot of emotion to spare for Paris, but I couldn't really blame him for that; he would have been used to dogs dying, after being involved with them for more than ten years. At the very least, though, it would have been nice if we'd been allowed to keep the harness—obviously not to use, but just as a reminder of the years that Paris had been my seeing-eye dog, and how she would try to dodge the harness when I went to put it over her head.

We got Paris's ashes back about a week after her death. I kept them beside my bed for a few weeks while I struggled with letting her go, but when I felt ready, I allowed them to be put in the family room instead. They were put in a crystal cabinet where they could be seen, beneath a shelf (because of course, Paris had always enjoyed squeezing beneath things in life).

My dad was thrilled when weeks later, he received a late birthday present from Molly – a large, framed charcoal sketch of Paris, drawn by my stepdad Stephen. He is an artist in his own right and can be located at **www.facebook.com/Stephen-Van-Duynhoven-Artist**. That sketch now hangs on the wall in the family room, where Paris can look down on us all.

My dad created his own tribute to Paris; a photo book packed with memories, not unlike this one, though with much less narrative. Rather than being told from our perspectives, he wrote it as though Paris were telling her own story. His book and mine were initially going to be one in the same, but writing this tribute story turned out to be more difficult than I had anticipated when I had first decided to do it. That decision had been made on the night of Paris's death, though I had been contemplating it for at least a week prior to that.

I still miss Paris, of course. I don't think I'll ever stop missing her, even when I eventually get a new seeing-eye dog. That dog, when I meet it, will also have a place in my heart, but it could never replace Paris. The paw print she left on all of our hearts is very much permanent.

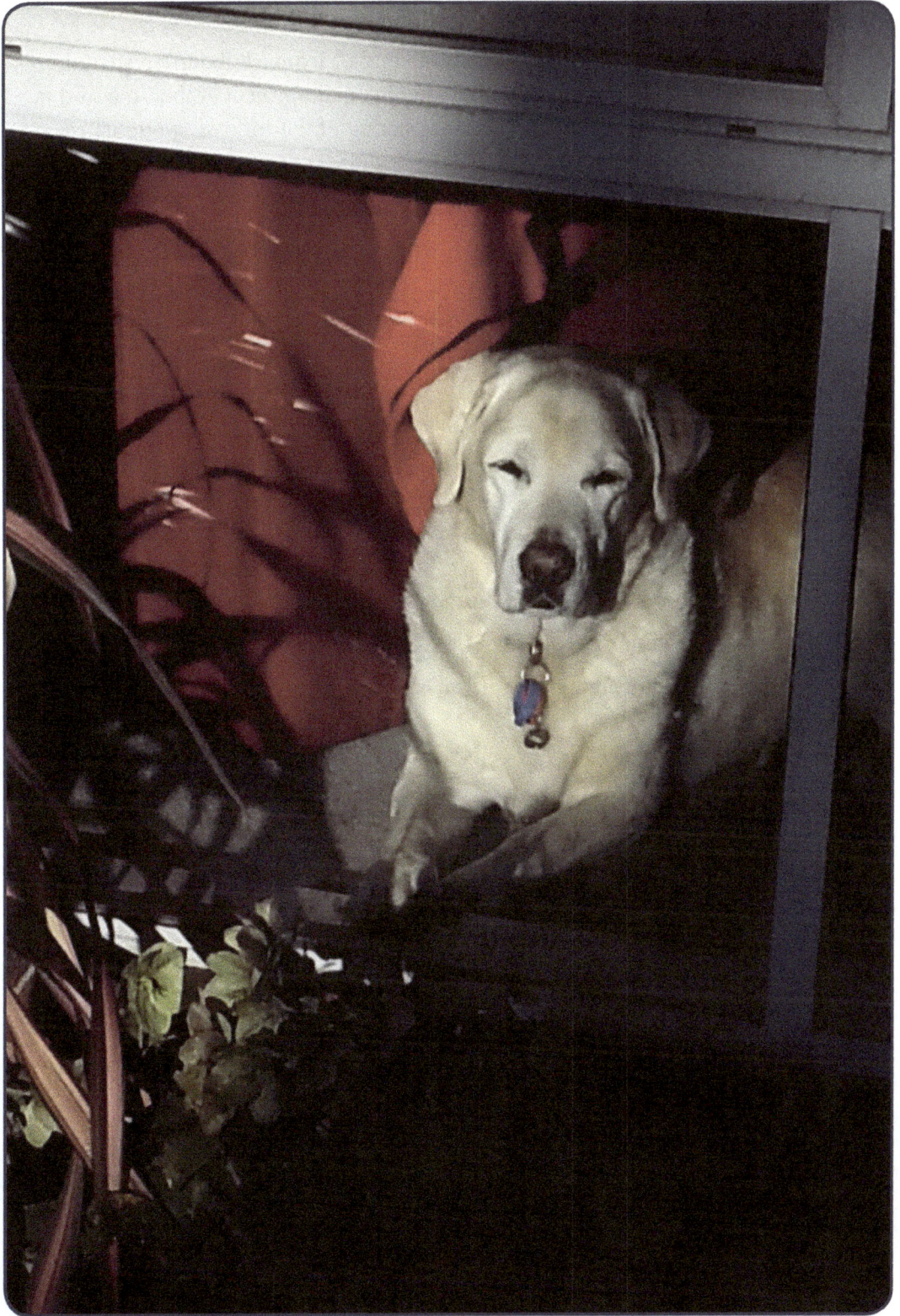

2016: Paris in her favourite spot through the day - looking out the front window watching the goings-on in the street outside.

ABOUT THE AUTHOR

Stephen Hayes, born in 1986, is a totally-blind author from Melbourne, Australia. Stephen usually writes in the fantasy genre and his main project at the time of this publication is the 'Magic Crystals' series, consisting of the following published books in print, ebook or audio book:

- Book 1: The Seventh Sorcerer (published in 2013)
- Book 2: Rock Haulter (published in 2013)
- Book 3: Hunt and Power (published in 2014)
- Book 4: Corridors (published in 2015)
- Book 5: The Cloak of Steel (to be published)
- Book 6: On the String (to be published)
- Book 7: TBA (to be published)

More information about Stephen Hayes can be found by following these links:

Official Website: **www.stephenhayesonline.com**

Facebook: **www.facebook.com/AuthorStephenHayes**

Twitter: **www.twitter.com/SteveTheHayes**

Goodreads: **www.goodreads.com/author/show/6927324.Stephen_Hayes**